Masai Mara
Mara Triangle

Official Guide

David Watson

Produced in collaboration with Mara Conservancy

Welcome from the Governor

"Welcome to the Mara Triangle, the western section of the Masai Mara National Reserve, the world's greatest game reserve. You may be surprised to learn that the Masai Mara is not a national park, run by the government, but is actually owned by the Maasai people of the area. As such it is run for the sustainable and mutual benefit of both wildlife and the people who live around it.

In many ways the Maasai were the original conservationists in East Africa. Unlike most other tribes, the Maasai did not hunt the wildlife, whose land they shared. Instead they lived side by side in harmony, a forerunner of today's more formal conservation arrangements.

The Mara Game Reserve, covering the area of the present Mara Triangle, was created in 1948, and in 1961 the Masai Mara National Reserve, more or less as we know it, was formed, with slight adjustments made in 1984. Since 2001, The Triangle, an area enclosed by the Oloololo Escarpment, the Mara River and the Tanzanian border, has been managed by Mara Conservancy.

The Mara Triangle is run on strict, sustainable conservation principles, allowing visitors to continue to enjoy one of the world's greatest wildlife spectacles, and for the Maasai people also to benefit by sharing its revenue. We thank you for choosing to visit the Mara Triangle. By doing so, your entrance fee, and the proceeds from this official guidebook, will be devoted to continuing the conservation effort."

Samuel Ole Tunai
Governor, Narok County

Contents

Introduction, and how to use this guide 2-3

1. Maps 4-7

2. Habitats of the Triangle 8-23

3. The Seasons 24-27

4. Animals of the Mara Triangle, frequently asked questions 28-33

5. Animal Checker 34-39

6. The Predators 40-47

7. Elephants, Rhinos and Buffalo 48-53

8. Birds 54-59

9. How to improve your wildlife watching 60-61

10. Park Rules 62-63

11. Some suggested game drives 64-81

12. The Great Migration 82-87

13. The Maasai and the Mara 88-93

14. Conservation and Management... 94-97

15. How to get there 98-99

16. Where to stay 100-105

17. Find out more 106

Acknowledgements 107

About the author 108

Your notes 109-110

INTRODUCTION

The Purpose of the Guidebook

This guide is to help you make the most of your visit, and afterwards to know that you have experienced the world's greatest wildlife reserve to the full.

Some of you will come with the aspiration of seeing the Big Five. All five are here, but we hope that this guide will show you that there is so much more to your visit than just the five top species. We want you to achieve a much more complete experience.

The Masai Mara National Reserve

The Masai Mara National Reserve is one of the world's greatest wildlife areas, and its present boundaries, enclosing just over 1500 km sq, were finalised in 1984. The first move to protect this as a special area was in 1948, when the Mara Triangle, an area of 520 km sq, was declared a National Game Reserve. Then in 1961 the area of the Reserve east of the Mara river was added, tripling the protected area. The boundaries were adjusted to their present locations in 1984.

THE MARA TRIANGLE

The Mara Triangle, often referred to as simply "the Triangle", is the western part of the Masai Mara National Reserve and is bounded by the Mara River on the east, Oloololo Escarpment to the west, and the border with Tanzania to the south. It is located in southwest Kenya, with Lake Victoria only about 90 km (56 miles) to the west. To get here you will probably have crossed the equator, so you are now in the southern hemisphere, at about 1° south, latitude. Nairobi is just under 300 km away (about 180 miles) and it takes about an hour by air, or about five hours by road to reach here.

How to use the guidebook

The guidebook is designed both for use in the field and also to give you a wider perspective before and during your safari.

The first half of the guide is very much hands-on, and is aimed at enhancing your actual safari experience. Amongst other information, it includes maps, explanations of habitats, an animal checker and the rules of the reserve.

The second half of the guide gives you more perspective on the relationship between the Maasai people and the Masai Mara, on the Great Migration, and how the Mara Triangle is managed and conserved.

This is one of the world's greatest wildlife experiences, and we hope you enjoy it.

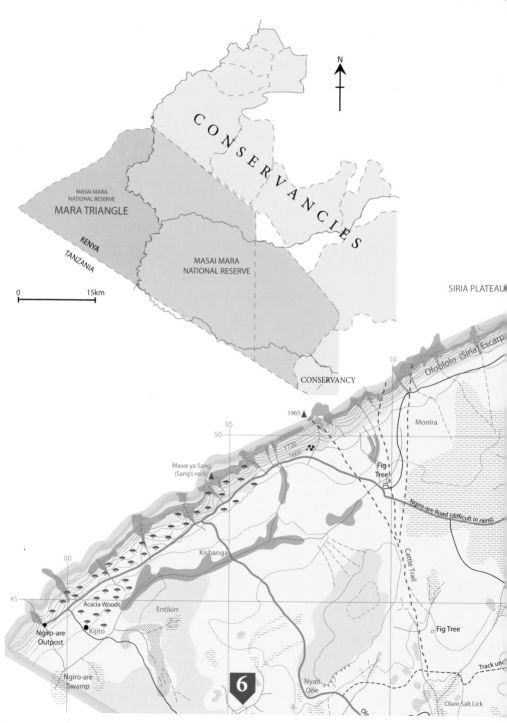

N

CONSERVANCIES

MASAI MARA
NATIONAL RESERVE
MARA TRIANGLE

KENYA
TANZANIA

0   15km

MASAI MARA
NATIONAL RESERVE

SIRIA PLATEAU

CONSERVANCY

10

Oloololo (Siria) Escarp

1965

Monira

05

50

1720

1600

Mawe ya Sang
(Sang's rock)

Fig
Tree

Ngiro-are Road (difficult in rains)

Kishanga

Cattle Trail

00

45

Acacia Woods

Entikirr

Fig Tree

Ngiro-are
Outpost

Kijito

Ngiro-are
Swamp

6

Nyati
One

Olare Salt Lick

Track und

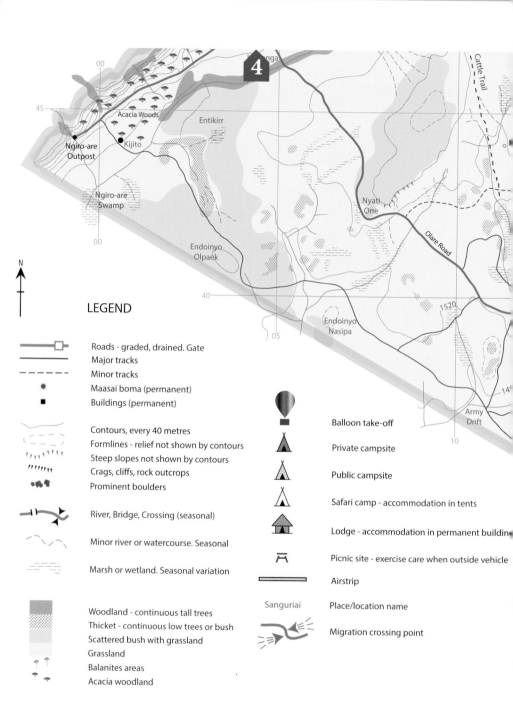

LEGEND

Roads - graded, drained. Gate	
Major tracks	
Minor tracks	
Maasai boma (permanent)	
Buildings (permanent)	
Contours, every 40 metres	
Formlines - relief not shown by contours	
Steep slopes not shown by contours	
Crags, cliffs, rock outcrops	
Prominent boulders	
River, Bridge, Crossing (seasonal)	
Minor river or watercourse. Seasonal	
Marsh or wetland. Seasonal variation	
Woodland - continuous tall trees	
Thicket - continuous low trees or bush	
Scattered bush with grassland	
Grassland	
Balanites areas	
Acacia woodland	

Balloon take-off

Private campsite

Public campsite

Safari camp - accommodation in tents

Lodge - accommodation in permanent building

Picnic site - exercise care when outside vehicle

Airstrip

Sanguriai   Place/location name

Migration crossing point

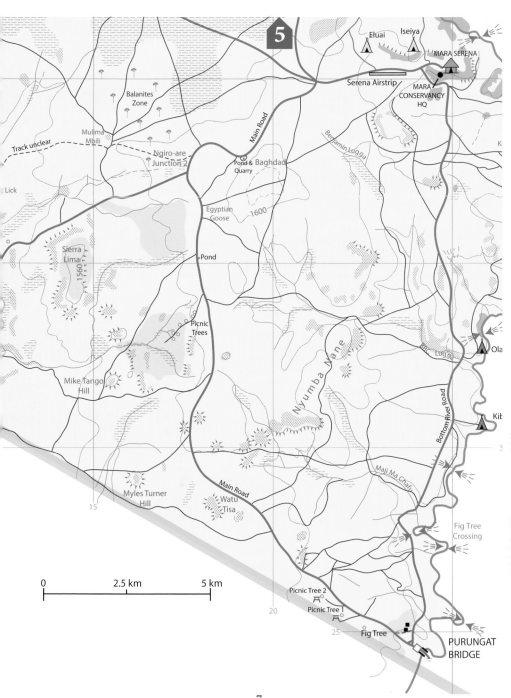

THE HABITATS OF THE MARA TRIANGLE

	Pages
The Mara River	10-12
Riverine Forest	13
Grasslands	14-15
Wetlands	16-17
Woodland & bush savanna	18-20
Thicket	21
Oloololo Escarpment	22
Inselberg country	23

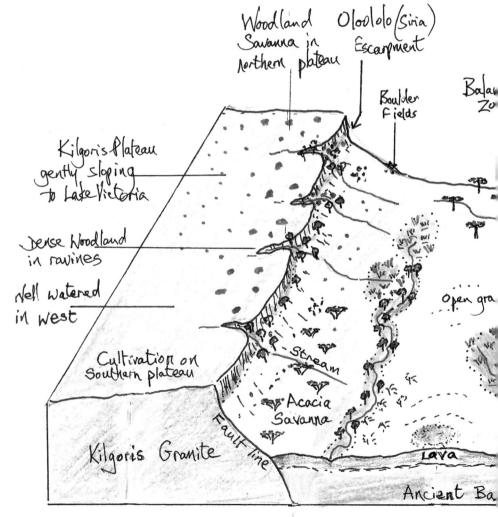

Woodland Savanna in northern plateau

Oloololo (Siria) Escarpment

Boulder Fields

Bala Zo

Kilgoris Plateau gently sloping to Lake Victoria

Dense Woodland in ravines

Well watered in west

Open gra

Cultivation on Southern plateau

Stream

Acacia Savanna

Fault Line

Kilgoris Granite

Lava

Ancient Ba

Appreciating the relationship between animals and their habitat is the most important key to understanding animal behaviour in the Mara Triangle.

Habitats result from a wide combination of factors, starting with the geology and soils, then the climate, especially variations in rainfall amount and frequency. The availability of surface water is another factor which affects vegetation, as are the influences of both other animals and man.

The result is a series of ecosystems, some of which exist largely on their own, and others which gradually merge into others, with no distinct boundaries.

FIELD SKETCH SHOWING TRIANGLE HABITATS

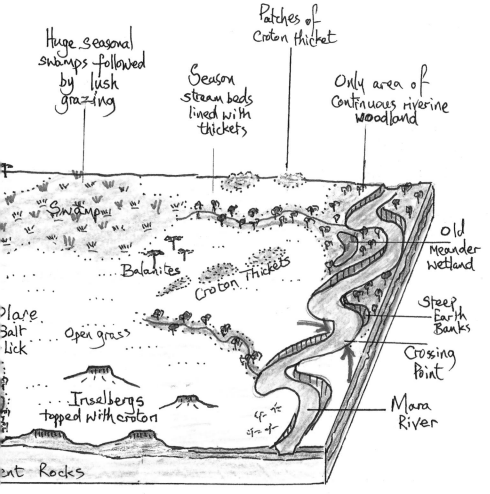

The Mara River

The Mara River flows from the forests of the Mau Escarpment and never dries up. So it is the most important single aspect of all the habitats in the Masai Mara. Varying from about 20m to 50-60m wide, it meanders mainly over a bed of alluvium, occasionally interrupted by bands of resistant dark-coloured rock which create little rapids. The river cuts deeply into the clay soil, creating sheer banks up to 10m which cause havoc during the migrations.

Originally a rich forest followed the river its entire way through the Triangle, with species such as the Yellow Barked acacia, called the Fever Tree by early European settlers, because they associated it with malaria. Today, the zone of continuous woodland is generally confined to the river banks north of Serena.

The river has a range of important functions. It is home to hundreds of hippo which spend the day in the water congregating in groups called "pods", and which leave the river to graze at night. And there are hundreds of huge Nile crocodile, often sunning themselves on the "beaches" in groups waiting for their next meal to arrive "on the hoof".

In the dry season, the river becomes the main water source, and so is the focus for many species such as elephant and buffalo, which come down to the water to drink.

Most dramatic for the visitor is the role played by the Mara River as an obstacle which must be crossed during the annual migrations, with thousands of wildebeest, zebra and even Thomson's gazelle taking to the river at a single time. (See Great Migration, pages 82-87)

The river and the forest around it is the main focus for Mara bird life, with over 500 recorded species.

Left: Meanders and woodland of the Mara River

Look for Nile crocodile up to 6 metres and **Hippo pods** all along the river.
Water birds include the African fish eagle, herons, egrets, storks, kingfishers and Egyptian geese.
Many animals come to drink including elephant, buffalo, and all the other water-dependent herbivores.
There are spectacular crossings with thousands of wildebeest, zebra and Thomson's gazelle, from July to October.

Above: Bend on the Mara river

HABITATS

Mara River

Riverine Forest

Sixty years ago most of the Masai Mara was either forested or mainly covered with bush and woodland savanna. Today forest is limited in the Triangle to a few areas of riverine woodland along the Mara river, between Serena and the Kichwa airstrip, around the upper Sanguraia river, and along the Ngiro-are river. Other small patches exist, often in deep ravines, along the Oloololo Escarpment.

Here we find a tree-storey including dense, continuous stands of Yellow-barked fever trees, Ugandan green-heart, and Phoenix palms.

Below is an under-storey of smaller bushes such as Grevia, Teclea and Orange-leaved croton.

Although the woodland is a habitat difficult for the visitor to access, nevertheless it is probably the home of more species than any other part of the Masai Mara, with over 500 species of birds alone.

Animal species
Look on the woodland edge for:
Buffalo
Elephant
Bush duiker
Bushbuck
Monkeys (Vervet, Copper-tailed and Sykes)
Bushbaby (More likely to hear them, at night)
Hyrax
And hundreds of bird species.

Tree Species
Warburgia ugandensis (Ugandan greenheart)
Acacia xanthophloea (Yellow-barked fever tree)
Phoenix reclinata (Phoenix palm)
Euclea divinorum
Dyospiros abyssinica
Olea europaea spp africana

Understorey Species
Grevia
Teclea
Croton dichogamus

Left: You will see huge pods of hippo in and out of the water.

Right: The forest typically has an upper storey of tall trees and an under-storey of smaller trees and bushes.

The Grassland Habitat

For most visitors, it is the grassland habitat which most appeals. A casual look suggests homogeneity, with rolling plains of red-oat grass going on forever. However, in reality, the grasslands are quite varied, and different areas are used by different grazers.
Grasslands vary from those on black cotton soils of marshes such as the seasonally-flooded Olpunyata swamp, to those of the lava-covered rolling Karoo plain. Some areas, such as along the middle section of the Tanzania border, are based on sandy and stony quartz-based soils. In some areas there can be considerable variation within a small area. (See page 23 on Inselbergs)

During the annual migrations the grasslands assume a special importance and undergo an amazing process. Following the March and April rains, with the grass tall and lush throughout the Mara, an almost locust-like invasion of two million wildebeest and zebra will soon reduce it to a dry stubble, removing every blade of fodder.
(See "The Great Migration" pages 82-87)

Selective Grazing

On close examination, it appears that grazers are not all eating the same grass, or at least grass at the same stage.

Buffalo are relatively unselective. Zebra can cope with coarser grasses. Wildebeest prefer new, green shoots. Gazelle prefer the new, short shoots of both grasses and herbs.

The main herbivores include:

Elephant, Buffalo, Wildebeest, Zebra Topi, Kongoni, Eland, Thomson's and Grant's gazelle and Warthog.

And there are the attendant predators, lion, cheetah, hyena and jackal.

The main grass species are:

Themeda triandra (Red oat grass, the most important)

Hyparrhenia rufa (Thatch grass)

Bothriochloa insculpa (Sweet pitted grass)

Amongst the grasses, especially in the Olpunyata area, are many small, flowering plants, herbs and low shrubs, which provide browsing for animals such as rhino.

Wetlands

During and immediately after the rains, vast areas in the Mara Triangle are either flooded or are very wet. During the intervening drier months, some of these wetlands remain, and it is possible to identify several types.

Wetlands

The commonest wetlands are those shown on the map with a marsh symbol (See pages 4-7). In general these are areas with a permanently high water-table, usually maintained by a stream which disappears and spreads out in the "swamp", eg. as with the Sanguraia stream. As you look over the plain in the dry season, although there may be little or no surface water, you can easily see the richer green of the grass in these places. Often there are herds of elephant scattered around them, enjoying the rich, juicy grass.

A second type of wetland can be found along the Mara river, where former meanders remain as "ox-bow lakes", large ponds flooded in the rains, which retain water most or all of the year. Many are hidden in the forest, but a few, such as that at Little Governors', are easily seen, and form the most beautiful and peaceful environment.
They attract a host of water birds such as egrets, herons and jacana, together with hippo, elephant, buffalo and bushbuck around the fringes.

Finally, there is a specialist wetland, where springs, laden with minerals, rise to the surface and may flow all year. The best known of these is Olare, (meaning "salt) in the southern Triangle. Wild herbivores (and in the past poachers) are attracted to the salty water, sometimes remaining just as a "salt lick". Every second Saturday, Maasai from the Kilgoris plateau above the escarpment, exercise their right to bring their cattle along well-worn trails, to drink the salty water. (See pages 76-77)

Left: Weed-covered wetland at Little Governors'
Left inset: Jacana

Above: After the rains, swamps dry out to lush grass much loved by elephants

Woodland and Bush Savanna

Savanna is mainly grassland, and with much the same range of animal species as grassland, but is also a landscape of scattered trees or bushes. These habitats have several, important functions. They provide food for many animals, both as browsing and from their fruits, and they create shade from the hot sun, much enjoyed by a range of species, from lion to elephant. In the Triangle there are several, distinct savanna habitats.

Balanites zone in northern Triangle

Balanite trees are distinctively scattered around the grassland within and both north and south of the Olpunyata swamp. This is an unusual landscape, only found in the Triangle. Balanites fruit are eaten by baboon, elephant, monkeys and impala.

One concern for the balanites trees is that all the trees are mature, with little evidence of young trees managing to survive. Elephant and other browsers give seedlings little chance. Clearly the present trees grew up at a time when the balance of germinating seeds and animals was quite different. One of the many challenges facing the management of the Reserve.

Giant fig trees are scattered around the Triangle

Woodland and Bush Savanna

In the far southwest of the Triangle, situated just below the escarpment slope, is a beautiful area of acacia savanna, especially of Acacia gerrrardii. It is an area rich in wildlife, especially elephant, which feed off the acacia, and sadly cause much damage, when grass is less available.

Savanna species
Savanna is mainly grassland, and so the animals are more or less grassland species. However, they will also include fruit eaters, such as baboon and monkeys, and also browsers such as giraffe and impala.

Acacia savanna in the southwest

Plant species include six common acacias
Acacia brevispica ("Wait a bit" thorn)
Acacia drepolobium (Whistling thorn)
Acacia gerrardii
Acacia hockii
Acacia senega
Acacia xanthophloae (Fever tree, early Europeans mistakenly associated the incidence of malaria with these trees).

Trees provide much needed shade

Woodland and Bush Savanna (continued)

In the extreme southwest, south of the Ngiro-are river is an area of acacia bush savanna, especially the distinctive whistling thorns.

Above: Whistling thorn galls with their protective ants

Whistling thorn foliage

The whistling thorn has a symbiotic relationship (a sort of "you scratch my back and I'll scratch yours") with a species of ants living in the "galls" found on the plant. Whenever you (or a browsing impala or giraffe) touches the plant, the ants come streaming out, spraying formic acid, to protect their home, and so also protecting the acacia.

Bushland or Thicket

Sixty years ago, most of the Masai Mara was covered in bushland or forest. Today, due to a combination of the damage by elephant and fire, these bushland areas are much reduced, and there is now open grassland. However, the bushand habitats which remain are an important habitat.

Now they tend to be found around the tops of the hills, and along the seasonal riverbeds. On your game drive, pay special attention to the thickets. During the day, more often than not, this may be where you will find lion and cheetah resting up.

Always check the thickets

Animal species include:
Black rhino, warthog, dik-dik, impala
Many animals use the bush for shade, especially lion, cheetah and buffalo.

Plant species include:
Croton dichogamus (Orange-leaved croton). Not a usual food plant, but providing fruits which are eaten by some animals, eg. baboon and impala.
Euclea divinorum (Ol-kinyei in Swahili)
Olea europaea spp Africana (Brown olive)
Euphorbia candelabrum (Candelabra tree)
Acacia brevispica
Teclea
Cordia monoica (sandpaper bush)
Terenna graveolens

Orange-leaf croton

21

Oloololo Escarpment

Forming the western boundary of the Masai Mara, one side of the Mara Triangle, is a continuous escarpment ranging from 160-200 metres in height. It runs along a geological faultline, a crack in the earth's surface, and forms the edge of a granite plateau, which stretches westwards to Lake Victoria. To the east is the Masai Mara, made up of the ancient rocks of Africa and partly covered with lava.

The Oloololo Escarpment is probably the least visited area in the Mara Triangle. However, it is rich in wildlife, and is well worth seeking out. Follow the Out of Africa track near the Oloololo Gate, and the track below the Escarpment from the Sanguraia Bridge south to Kilo 2, or the road to the anti-poaching outpost near the Tanzanian border. Or you might see it from the top, as at Mara West camp, just outside the Reserve.

Cliffs, ravines and forest at the top give way to savanna and boulder fields at the base.

The habitats are mixed, but the Escarpment generally receives more rain than the rest of the Triangle, and is well-watered, with plenty of grass. There are lots of springs with fresh water, and lots of little lush-green wetlands, where streams disappear into the ground, but maintain a high water-table. These are especially favoured by elephant, eg. between Sanguraia bridge and the Oloololo gate.

You might reasonably expect species which are attracted to rocky places to be resident on the slopes, the klipspringer, hyrax, baboon and leopard, and they are all there. In addition there are deep, shaded ravines enjoying almost rainforest conditions, for example in the incised valleys above the Sanguraia bridge, and high on the slopes further southwest.

So you find a whole range of species, from eland and buffalo, to elephant and giraffe, and not many visitors.

Zebra and impala grazing near the top of the escarpment below Mara West camp.

Inselberg country

The final habitat we identify is a combination of several of the habitats already described.
In the south of the Triangle, mainly between the Ngiro-are road and the Main road, is an area
of little hills, called "inselbergs", meaning "island hills".
The hills, which are 70-100m high, are flat-topped and the summit is largely covered with
thicket. Mostly they have a steep, upper slope, which gradually becomes more gentle as it
reaches the valley floor.
The tops of the hills are usually rocky, with occasional crags, and the upper slopes are stony,
with short, thin grass. The lower slopes have taller grass, and often the valley bottom is a
seasonal swamp, with a permanently high water-table enabling green, moisture-rich grass for
much of the year.
The result of this little combination of landscapes is that within quite small areas, we see a
range of wildlife adapting to quickly changing conditions, and each having their own slot in
the ecosystem.

This is a habitat where you might park up and stay a while.

Animal species include:
Dik-dik and klipspringer in the rocky thickets at the top.
Impala on the short grass and close to the browsing near
the summit.
Other grazers including elephant, zebra, topi and eland in
the longer, more lush grasses in the valley.

The Seasons in the Masai Mara

The year in the Mara Triangle is punctuated by the seasons, two periods of rain, the Long Rains and the Short Rains, with dry seasons, times of drought, in between.
Some animals are year-long residents in the Mara, but others, mainly the wildebeest and zebra, respond to the changes in rainfall and vegetation to create the world's greatest annual migration of large mammals. This chapter describes the climatic reasons for the changes in the Triangle throughout the year.

Masai Mara: rainfall and temperature

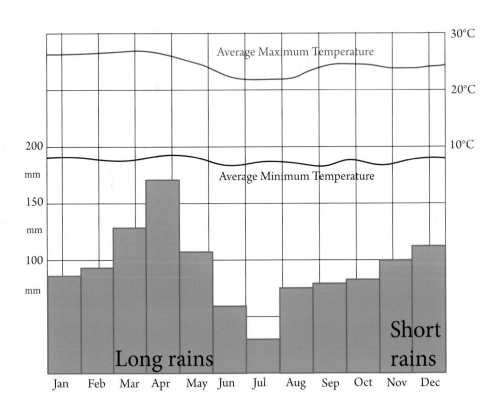

Rainfall: monthly average in millimetres

January-February, the start of the year

The Short Rains are over, and the Mara is green. There may be occasional scattered showers, but it is largely dry. This is the hottest time of the year, with daytime temperatures up to 30°C. The migrations are five months away, but there are still lots of animals. All the predators, lion, leopard, cheetah, and hyena are still here, now hunting the resident herbivores, which live in the Triangle all year.

The Mara is the only one of the main rivers still flowing. Most streams have disappeared, with others reduced to a string of pools or vanishing into the marshes.

Not all the wildebeest and zebra go "walkabout" to Serengeti, and some large herds remain. There are also still loads of gazelle, both Thomson's and Grant's.
Elephant are largely resident, as are big herds of buffalo, eland, impala and topi. At this time lions favour the abundant warthog.

Seasonal rivers become a succession of pools in the dry season

March-April-May, the Long Rains

The rains begin in March, peak in April and are over by the end of May. They transform the landscape. The usually languid Mara River becomes a torrent; watercourses fill to their brim in hours, and the areas named "marsh" on the map become lakes. Much of the Mara becomes impassable, camps close up, and there are few tourists.

But the rains bring the magic and refreshment to this land. In his book "The Marsh Lions", Brian Jackman describes the almost springtime effect "....when the whole country seemed to shine with a kind of new-minted freshness, and every plain, lugga, marsh and hollow buzzed, seethed and pulsed with life."

This is the time when the grass grows, in preparation for one of nature's most spectacular events, the Great Migration.

Mara river in flood at Purungat Bridge

June-October, the Great Migration (also see pages 82-87)

The annual migration of wildebeest and zebra begins far to the south in the short-grass plains of the southern Serengeti. The herds approach from the south and the east and by the end of June begin to spill out into the Triangle and the vast plains east of the Mara river.
It is the time of plenty, and over two or three months the raiders from the south concentrate on mowing down the tall oat grass until it becomes a dusty stubble, and the predators have supper walking on to their "plate" every day.
For the visitor it is the time of unbelievable numbers of animals, and for the spectacle of the Mara River crossing by thousands of animals.
July is the driest month, the plains become dusty, and it will not rain much until October.

Mara River crossing

October-December, quiet again

By October, the grass is all gone, mowed down by 2 million mouths. The land is suffering from five months with little or no rain, and the herds begin to head south to Tanzania. Soon they are gone, and the Mara is left to the resident animals. But not all the wildebeest and zebra migrate, and there are still substantial herds remaining. Many animals, such as buffalo, topi, impala and eland remain within their home range, and although elephant do move between the grassland to the acacia woodland, they often occur in huge herds. All the predators remain; they do not follow the herds as some writers would have you believe.
In November the short rains bring their rejuvenating moisture, and the grass, now fertilised by the dung of two million extra animals, begins to grow again. By the end of the year the plains are again a sea of tall oat grass.

ANIMALS OF THE MARA TRIANGLE

Frequently asked Questions

Which animals live here all the time (residents)?

Which animals move around (migrants)?

How do animals relate to one another?

How do they all find enough to eat?

Are they all competing for food?

Which are the predators, and which the prey?

Resident or Migrant?
Fortunately for the visitor, most animals are resident. They also have a "home range", and do not venture far from it. Home ranges vary greatly between species but, for the visitor, there are always thousands of animals in the Triangle.
A few, notably wildebeest, zebra, gazelle, and to a lesser extent eland, are the main players in the Great Migration. These are discussed mainly in chapter 12.
Some, such as Thomson's gazelle, have both resident and migrant populations.

Wildebeest and zebra two of the main migrant species

Home range

Probably the smallest home range is that of the dik-dik, where a pair of animals may stay within one square kilometre. Herds of female impalas may never venture outside a 2 - 6 square kilometre range, and others, such as duiker, bushbuck, reedbuck and oribi are also highly territorial.
The ubiquitous warthog has a range from about 0.6 - 3.0 square kilometres, but must include access to water.

Within the Mara Triangle, black rhino tend to remain within one fairly small area extending to a few square kilometres, but in some other places, territories may be several hundred square kilometres. Most important is access to water, as rhino need to drink every day.
Giraffe may go walkabout over large areas, but where there is adequate food, some will always be highly sedentary.

Warthog are found everywhere

Black rhino need daily access to water

Home range (continued)

Large animals have greater demands for food, so they often need to forage over wide areas. However, access to water will always be an important factor.

Elephants are always present in the Masai Mara, but they may travel within a huge area, from season to season, sometimes feeding mainly on grass, and at other times principally browsing.

Buffalo generally stay within a kilometre or two of water, but especially during the dry season may travel further for better grazing. In the Masai Mara, because of the good availability of grazing, the home range tends not to exceed ten square kilometres.

Elephant can have a home range of thousands of square kilometres

Wildebeest and zebra are the main migrant species

Eland males remain in smaller territories

Studies on **eland** show that the females and young tend to go walkabout over a large area, but that the males remain in smaller territories.

Topi appear to show a mixture of habits. Males tend to occupy a small home range, and there may be groups of males and females which jointly defend a home range. However, others use a wider home range. Their seasonal movement is affected by rains, as topi tend to favour flood plains.

Kongoni are largely fairly sedentary, but use a wider range in the dry season.

There is more on the main migrants in chapter 12, The Great Migration.

Social life of animals

To the casual observer, herds of wild animals live in a fairly chaotic mixture. However, in reality this is far from the case. This section looks at how some of the herbivores, the grazers, organise their lives.

The herd is all female apart from one male

For **impalas**, it is easy to see. Herds are either all female (no horns) with only one male, or alternatively all male (all with horns). Males are highly territorial and during the mating period, called the "rut", will try to maintain a harem within their territory. This is highly difficult, especially with a large harem, and other males are constantly patrolling on the edges of the group.
Outside the rut, male impalas seem to happily live in bachelor herds.

Topi are the iconic Triangle species

Topis are the iconic species to the Mara Triangle, and their social organisation is both distinctive and complicated.
Topi breeding herds vary in size. Males will seasonally defend a territory, marking it with scent glands and dung, and keep a lookout on a prominent place such a termite mound. They will then hope to mate with females entering their territory. Females mate after only 18 months, but males may be 4-5 years old.
Buffalo live in herds which assume a joint responsibility for defence. The herd is made up of females and young, together with active, mating males. Old bulls eventually leave the herd to live out their old age alone, or in small batchelor groups.
Buffalo do not defend a territory but groups may exclusively use a home area range.

Buffalo herds may have several hundred animals

Do all herbivores eat the same food?

Looking at a mixed herd of herbivores, you might wonder how they all get fed, and to a large extent the answer is that they do not all eat the same food.
Clearly giraffe have no competition when browsing up to 5 metres, but with lower range trees such as the acacias in the southwestern Triangle, elephant will be after the same food.
Impala are browsers **and** grazers, eating both grass and shoots of trees and bushes.
Black rhino are totally browsers, eating leaves in the thickets, and small shrubs and herbs on the ground, especially in the Olpunyata swamp.

The Grazing Succession
Some species such as zebra will eat the coarser grasses and seeds, whereas others, such as the wildebeest, prefer to come after the zebra, to eat the green, protein-rich grasses which are then exposed. So zebra and wildebeest often feed together, to the advantage of the latter.
Once the grass is mowed down, Thomson's gazelle can reach the lower, new-grown grasses and low herbs which they favour.

A few animals are in competition, such as buffalo and zebra, but there is generally enough grass to go round so this is not a problem.

Giraffes have no competition at this height

Zebra and wildebeest often graze together

32

Which prey for which predator?

It is the inevitable fate of all animals in the Masai Mara to be eaten.
Large predators will take larger animals and small predators smaller animals.
Then, at the end of the day, a range of scavengers, from hyena to jackal and vultures, will clean up.
At the top of the food chain, lion prey on wildebeest and zebra when they are available, mainly July to October, and on warthog, buffalo and a range of antelope outside the migration season.

A large pride has killed a wildebeest

Cheetah are limited to smaller prey, such as the gazelle and hare, but also the young of some larger animals.

Leopard are opportunistic and take prey from a wide range of small animals, ranging from dik-diks, Thomson's gazelle, warthog and impala, to the young of larger animals, such as such as zebra and wildebeest.

This leopard took its prey into the tree for safekeeping

Spotted hyena, once mainly regarded as scavengers around other kills, are now regarded as successful predators in their own right, and able to hunt a wide range of prey.

Wild dogs, though extremely rare, are once again seen in the Triangle. They are amongst the most efficient hunters, with the highest percentage of kills per attempt of all the large predators.
Their food range is extremely wide.
They are seen especially on the Oloololo Escarpment.

Spotted hyena, hunter and scavenger

" The Big Five "

	Common Name Swahili name	Scientific name	Height to shoulder	Mainly active by day/night
	Lion Simba	*Panthera leo*	1.0m	☀☾
	Leopard Chui	*Panthera pardus*	70cm	☾
	Black rhino Kifaru	*Diceros bicornis*	1.6m 🍃	☾
	Elephant Tembo/Ndovu	*Loxodonta africana*	up to 4m 🌾🍃	☀☾
	Buffalo Nyati	*Syncerus caffer*	1.0m 🌾🍃	☀☾

Other common predators

	Common name *Swahili name*	Scientific name	Height to shoulder	Mainly active by day/night
	Black-backed jackal *Bweha*	*Canis mesomelas*	40cm	☀️🌙
	Cheetah *Duma*	*Acinonyx jubatus*	75-78cm	☀️
	Crocodile *Mamba*	*Crocodius niloticus*	to 6.0m length	☀️
	Spotted hyena *Fisi*	*Hyaena hyaena*	70-85cm	🌙

Grazers and Browsers

Herbivores eat plants and can be divided into "grazers", eating mainly grass,

and "browsers", eating leaves, bark, shrubs and legumes.

Other animals may both graze and browse.

Some animals eg. buffalo only browse when grass is scarce.

ANIMAL CHECKER

Other large or common animals you should see

	Common Name / Swahili Name	Scientific Name	Height to Shoulder	Mainly active day/night
	Banded mongoose / Kicheche	Mungos mungo	20cm / 50-65cm length	☀ 🌙
	Burchell's zebra / Punda milia	Equus burchelllii	1.5m	☀ 🌙
	Coke's hartebeest / Kongoni	Alcelaphus buselaphus cokii	1.5 m	☀
	Common duiker / Nyasa	Sylvicapra grimmia	45-60cm	☀
	Defassa waterbuck / Kuro (Kuru)	Kobus ellipsiprymnus defassa	120-135cm	☀
	Eland / Mpunga	Tragelaphus oryx	1.6m	☀ 🌙
	Grant's gazelle / Swala granti	Gazella grantii	75-90cm	☀
	Hippopotamus / Kiboko	Hippopotamus amphibius	1.5m	☀ 🌙 day in river : feed at night
	Impala / Swala pala	Aepyceros melampus	75-90cm	☀ 🌙

36

Other large or common animals you should see

	Common Name / Swahili Name	Scientific Name	Height to Shoulder	Mainly active day/night
	Kirk's Dik-dik / Dik dik	*Modoqua kirkii*	35-40cm	☀
	Masai Giraffe / *Twiga*	*Camelopardilis tippelskirchi*	Up to 5.0m	☀
	Olive Baboon / Nyani	*Papio cynocephalus anubis*	1.5m	☀
	Ostrich / Mbuni	*Struthio camelus*	1.7-2.8m	☀
	Thompson's gazelle / Swala tomi	*Gazella thomsonii*	70cm	☀
	Topi / Nyamera	*Damaliscus lunatus jimela*	100-130cm	☀
	Vervet monkey / Tumbili	*Cercopithecus aethiops*	42-49cm	☀
	Warthog / Ngiri	*Phacochoerus africanus*	75cm	☀
	White-bearded wildebeest / Nyumbu	*Conochaetes taurinus*	1.5m	☀☾

Species less common or more difficult to see

	Common Name *Swahili Name*	Scientific Name	Height to Shoulder	Mainly active day/night
	African honey badger (ratel) *Nyegere*	*Mellivora copensis*	35cm	☾
	African hare *Sungura*	*Lepus microtis*	Body length up to 60cm	☀
	African wild dog *Mbwa mwitu*	*Lycaon pictus*	75cm	☀ ☾
	Aardvark *Mhanga*	*Orycteropus afer*	60cm	☾
	Aardwolf *Fisi ya nkole*	*Proteles cristatus*	50cm	☾
	Bat-eared fox *Bewaha masigio*	*Otocyon magalotis*	35-40cm	☾
	Fruit bat *Popobawa*	*Eidolon helvum*	up to 1m wingspan	☾
	Bushbaby *Komba*	*Galago senegalensis*	16cm length	☾
	Caracal *Simbamangu*	*Felis caracal*	38-50 cm	☾
	Cape Pangolin *Kakakuona*	*Manis temminckii*	35-60cm length	☾
	Common bushbuck *Pongo*	*Tragelaphus scriptus*	70-89 cm	☀ ☾
	Common genet *Kanu*	*Genetta genetta*	86-105cm length	☾

Species less common or more difficult to see

	Common Name *Swahili Name*	Scientific Name	Height to Shoulder	Mainly active day/night
	Common reedbuck *Tohe milima*	*Redunca arundinum*	100-135cm	
	Dwarf mongoose *Nguchiro*	*Helogale Parvula*	18-28cm length	
	Bush hyrax *Pimbi*	*Heterohyrax brucei*	20cm	
	Klipspringer *Mbuzi mawe*	*Oreotragus oreotragus*	58cm	
	Leopard tortoise *Kobe*	*Geochelone pardilis*	Up to 70cm length	
	Marsh Mongoose *Kicheche*	*Atilax paludinosus*	45-60cm length	
	Monitor lizard *Kamusi*	*Veranus niloticus*	120-160cm length	
	Syke's Monkey *Kima/nchima*	*Cercopithecus mitis*	40-50cm	
	Oribi *Taya*	*Ourebia ourebi*	50-65cm	
	Serval cat *Mondo*	*Felis serval*	55-65cm	
	Side-striped jackal *Bweha*	*Canis adustus*	45-50cm	
	Porcupine *Nungunungu*	*Hystrix africanaeaus- tralis*	60-90cm	

LION

Lion: *Panthera leo* (Swahili: *Simba*)
Length:males 1.7-2.5m; females 1.6-1.0m
Height: male 1.3m; females 1.1m
Male weight: 150-240kg
Female weight:120-180kg

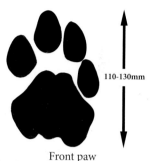

110-130mm

Front paw

Social behaviour

Lion prides are made up of related adult females and their young, together with an unrelated pride male or a coalition of males. Females will generally stay with the pride all their lives, but adolescent males are expelled at about two years old. The females generally hunt together and look after their young communally.

When a new male or coalition takes over a pride, usually by fierce fighting, the incoming male(s) will kill all existing cubs and sub-adults. The females quickly come into season, mate with the new male or males, and then have their cubs all at about the same time. In order for a generation of cubs to survive to adulthood, each pride needs to remain stable, with the same male, for about two and a half years.

The Masai Mara is famous for its lion, often having amongst the highest lion densities in Africa.
They are the only truly social big cats, living in "prides" which range in numbers from around four adults to occasionally over thirty.

Above: Two lionesses enjoyng the shade
Left: Large pride male

41

PREDATORS OF THE MARA TRIANGLE

Lion core pride areas

Lion tend to have a core pride area where the females usually live most of their lives. Only the males move around much.

The Mara Triangle has about seven identifiable core pride areas, which are shown on the map. *Oloololo Pride*, in the northern Triangle, the most stable pride.

Sausage Pride, named after a sausage tree, along the central escarpment.

Mogoro Pride in the Olpunyata Swamp.

Serena Pride, from Serena southwards.

Egyptian Goose Pride astride the Main Road going south.

Purungat Pride in the southeast corner.

Border Pride, overlaps the Tanzania border.

Food

Lion are the top carnivores. They kill a variety of prey, such as wildebeest, zebra and warthog, so providing food not only for themselves, but also for such scavengers as hyena, jackal and vultures. During the migration (July - Nov) they feed mainly on wildebeest and zebra. The rest of the time their favourite is warthog, but they take a range of antelope and also buffalo.

Lion usually, but not exclusively, hunt at night, most often in co-operating groups of pride members, normally females.

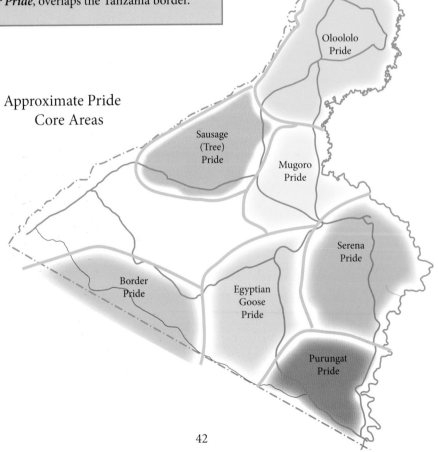

Approximate Pride Core Areas

Trouble in the Triangle

A healthy pride of lion depends mainly on having a pride male, or a coalition of males who are strong enough to protect the pride from a take-over by the unattached males who patrol the Masai Mara. It takes two and a half years for cubs sired by a pride male to become adult, and safe from the attack of a new male takeover.

Before about 2009, the Mara Triangle lion were very stable. However, from then on a disturbing pattern began. On the east side of the Mara river is the strongest coalition of male lion ever seen in the Masai Mara in recent times. A powerful lion called Notch has been joined by his three sons (originally there were four) and they are able to take on all-comers. All very well if they keep to their own side of the river.

However, in the last few years, Notch and his team have crossed the river repeatedly, chasing off pride males, killing all cubs and sub-adults, and mating with the females. If they then stayed, all would be well, with strongly-defended prides. But Notch and his boys do not stay long. Instead they again cross the river to their home territory, and the prides are then vulnerable to further takeovers and the killing of cubs.

Only the Oloololo pride in the northern Triangle has remained stable. The rest have been vulnerable for several years.

The solution lies either in new, strong coalitions of males within the Triangle (one male lion is not enough to hold a pride for long), or the demise of Notch and his gang.

At the time of writing, Notch has gone missing. Check Facebook (see page 106) for updates.

Notch and sons sleeping after a kill

LEOPARD

Leopard: *Panthera pardus* (Swahili: *Chui*)
Length:100-190 cm; tail 70-90 cm
Height: 45-80 cm
Male weight: 30-70 kg
Female weight: 28-60 kg

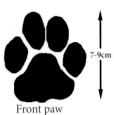

7-9cm

Front paw

Social life

Leopard only come together for mating, and mothers spend much of their lives looking after cubs. However, the rest of the time, and generally for males, leopards live a solitary life.

Females usually have a den amongst boulders or in cliffs, often on the bank of a river or seasonal water-course. Males in Kenya have a home range up to 30 km sq, whereas the female home range is up to about 12 km sq.

Leopard are probably the most adaptable of the big cats. They manage to survive in a wide variety of habitats. In the Triangle look for them everywhere apart from on open grassland.

Leopard are stealthy hunters, creeping close to their prey before launching an attack. Prey is highly varied, including small mammals, reptiles and birds. During the migration, the young of wildebeest and zebra are taken. Often an ambush is made from a very short distance.

Prey is often moved to a convenient nearby tree, to prevent scavenging hyena and lion from stealing it. Male leopard hunt on average every three days, females more often than that.

Male leopard hunting

44

CHEETAH

Cheetah: *Acinonyx jubatus* (Swahili: *Duma*)
Length: 110-135cm; tail 65-85cm.
Height: 90cm
Male weight: 43kg
Female weight: 38 kg.

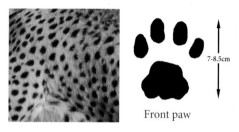

7-8.5cm

Front paw

Social life
Cheetah are the next most sociable big cats after lion. Siblings often stay together for perhaps 6 months after leaving their mother, and brothers often remain together for life. Male coalitions are common, with 30% of coalitions being of unrelated males. Females are solitary, with a home range which can be very large, up to 800 km sq, depending on prey numbers. Litters may be as large as eight, but there is a very high death rate, mainly from lion, hyena and baboon.

The cheetah is the fastest mammal on the planet, reaching speeds of up to 87km per hour, for two to three hundred metres, achieved because of an extremely flexible spine, and long, balancing tail.

Food
Unlike other big cats, cheetah eat only what they catch. They hunt almost entirely during the day, usually gazelle and small antelope which feed on short grass. Thomson's gazelle are the most popular.
Cheetah must eat quickly, as scavengers such as hyena and lion are quickly on the scene, and most kills are eventually stolen.

Cheetah mother and cub resting in the shade of a termite mound

HYENA

Hyena: *Crocuta crocuta (*Swahili: *Fisi)*
Length: 1.3-1.9m
Height: 45-80 cm
Male weight: 45-62 kg
Female weight: 55-82 kg
Hyena reputedly have the strongest jaws in the animal kingdom.

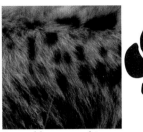

9-10.5cm

Spotted hyena markings   Front paw

Food

Hyena are hunters and scavengers, and are highly efficient at both. Often hunting in groups, they can bring down large prey such as wildebeest. Similarly a large clan of hyena can drive a large pride of lion from a kill, sometimes not without danger to both.

Hyena eat very quickly, with jaws equal to almost anything. They prey on animals across the entire range and can demolish a large animal such as a zebra in less than thirty minutes.

Some interesting facts about hyena
* Hyena clans can number up to 100 animals.
* Hyena society is controlled by a hierarchy of females. The highest ranked male is ranked below the lowest female.
* Hyena were at one time thought to be hermaphrodite. This is because externally the genitals of male and female look very similar.
* A large hyena clan can drive off a large lion pride from a kill.
* Although they look more like dogs, hyena are closely related to cats.

Hyena family

Researchers from Michigan State University have been studying Mara hyenas since 1998. For Masai Mara Hyena Project: www.msuhyenas.blogspot.com

Hyena society is highly structured. They live in groups, usually called clans, where young females inherit the clan position of their mother.

Females dominate. The highest ranking male is lower in the hierarchy than the lowest ranking female. Moreover females are more aggressive than males and normally stay with the clan for life, but males are pushed out at two and a half years old.

The home range of a clan averages about 65sq km, but it is not uncommon for some hyena to travel vast distances for food. Because of the richness of hyena milk, the young are able to go longer between feeds than most animals, and so the mother can forage further.

CROCODILE

Nile Crocodile: *Crocodylus niloticus*
(Swahili: *Mamba*)
Length: average 3.5-5.0m; occasionally 6.0m
Height: 45-80cm
Weight: 225-550kg.

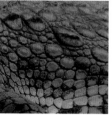

Crcodile hide   Front foot

The Nile crocodile is the second biggest reptile after the saltwater crocodile. Surviving since the age of the dinosaurs, crocodiles are extremely adaptable.
There are crocodiles all along the Mara river, and also on the tributary streams which retain pools throughout the dry season. In the river, they are the top predator. They are not an endangered species.

Food
Crocodiles are opportunist, ambush feeders. Although their ambush of wildebeest and zebra during the migration is perhaps the best known, they also take a wide range of other animals, including fish, reptiles and birds. In general, the larger the crocodile, the larger the chosen prey.
Crocodiles have a metabolism which allows them to go very long periods without eating. One wildebeest, for example, can last them for weeks, even months.

Social life
Crocodiles are very sociable, and spend much of their day basking in groups on sand-banks or on the edge of rivers.
Upstream from Serena on the Mara river, it is possible to see large groups of these animals. Their society is hierarchical, with the largest males being dominant. The females lay eggs in sand above the waterline, and they will fiercely defend their nest. Young are about 30cm when hatched and immediately seek out their own food.

Nile crocodile near the Hippo Pool

ELEPHANT

Elephant: *Loxodonta africana* (Swahili: *Tembo*)
Male height: 3.3m
Female height: 2.7m
Male weight: 6 tons
Female weight: 3 tons
The largest recorded African elephant stood about 4 metres, and weighed 10 tons.

Eyelashes to die for?

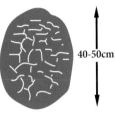
40-50cm

Elephant front footprint

Social Life
The elephant is one of the most social of all large mammals.

They live in herds of related females and their young. Adolescent males are forced to leave the herd before maturity, and they then live on their own or in bachelor groups. Mature males only join the herd for mating.

Each group of elephants is under the control and experience of a dominant, large and mature female.

Elephants communicate by sounds, 60% of which are below the normal human range.

Calves are born to females every three to four years, and the gestation period at 22 months, is the longest of any mammal.

Elephants in the Mara
There are about 3000 elephants in the Masai Mara ecosystem, occupying all habitats, and migrating between the National Reserve, Serengeti and the new conservancies.

However, until very recently, not a lot was known about their movements between the Kenyan and Tanzanian reserves. During the main wildebeest migration period, July to October, elephants are more likely to be found in the croton thickets and acacia woodlands, as they appear to avoid the hordes of visiting wildebeest, probably because the grasslands are reduced to a short "lawn". At other times they are everywhere, sometimes in family groups of twelve to fifteen, and sometimes in very large herds. After the rains they appear to highly favour the juicy grass of the seasonal swamp areas.

Elephants are integral to the Masai Mara habitat, not least due to the destruction they cause to woodland and bushland. Apart from uncontrolled fire, elephants are probably the main agents which, over the last 50 years, have changed the Reserve from a mainly wooded park to one which is now mainly grassland.

Grass is one of the main elephant foods

48

Elephants are very protective of their young

Some facts to know about elephants

Elephants can survive in almost any habitat, from rain-forest to desert.

The life-cycle of an elephant is very similar to that of humans. For example, male elephants only stay with the herd until they are "teenagers", about 12-15 years, when they are pushed out. Daughters usually stay with Mum all their lives.

Mum is boss. The herd is led by a mature female. The males only appear for mating.

Elephants eat 5% of their own body-weight per day, ad they can drink 200 litres of water at one time.

Normally they sleep standing up, a maximum of about 5 hours a day.

Elephants communicate with very low, subsonic vibrations, which can travel for miles, and which elephants can detect with their feet.

Elephants start to breed anything from 8 to 20 years. Gestation takes almost two years.

Finally, the life of an elephant is controlled by its teeth. Once the last of their six sets of molars is worn down, elephants find it difficult to find adequate sustenance, and they die aged about sixty.

ELEPHANTS OF THE MARA TRIANGLE

The Mara Elephant Project

After a period of relative security, elephants in Africa are again under threat, mainly from poachers feeding the demand for ivory which comes from southeast Asia in particular. In addition, agriculture is expanding around the fringes of the Masai Mara, sometimes cutting traditional elephant migration routes. Conflict with farmers is a constant problem. Perhaps 100 elephants are killed on the African continent every day.

The Mara Elephant Project was started in 2011. The principal aim is to track the elephants constantly in order to understand their movements, the migration corridors they need, and to improve security, allowing rapid response to anything unusual.

In December 2011, five females and five males were fitted with satellite tracking collars, allowing monitors to record elephant positions hourly. When unusual behaviour is noted, such as an elephant stopping moving or perhaps entering an area of crops, a rapid response team is dispatched.

Elephants, even in the monitored group, are still being killed, but hopefully the project will enhance both understanding and greater protection for the elephants of the Mara.

The Mara Elephant Project is partly funded by
ESCAPE Foundation.
https://www.facebook.com/ESCAPE fdn

Elephant with radio collar

BUFFALO

Buffalo: *Syncerous caffer*
(Swahili: *Nyati*)
Length: 2.1-3.4m
Height: 1-1.7m
Weight: up to 900kg
Africa's only "cattle"
species

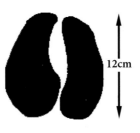

12cm

Front hoof

An old bull

Food
Buffalo have an important ecological slot. They are basically grass eaters, and are able to open up long grass areas, making them usable to species preferring short grass, such as wildebeest and the gazelles.
Buffalo need to have access to water, within about 3km, and they usually drink in the morning. During the heat of the day, they are often found in the shade of thickets, or in woodland.

Predators
An adult buffalo is a formidable adversary, so lion and hyena usually prey only on young animals. However, a large, well-organised lion pride is well capable of hunting mature buffalo, especially outside the migration season. Old and infirm animals will be targeted first.

Social Life
African buffalo are highly gregarious, often forming huge herds. There is a very strong bond between females and their calves, and the herd employs a communal defence against predators. Buffalo are more than able to drive off a pride of lions. Old bulls are usually solitary or may form small bachelor herds.

Finding shade in the croton thicket

RHINO

Rhino: *Diceros bicornis* (Swahili: *Kifaru*)
Length: 2.9-3.1m
Height: 1.3-1.6m
Weight: up to 800-1400kg
Life expectancy 25-50 years.

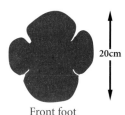

Front foot

Rhino numbers in the Masai Mara

1960s	Approx. 150
1970	Approx. 120
1984	18
1994	35
1999	23
Today	20-25

Black Rhino

The rhino in the Masai Mara are "Black" rhino as opposed to "White" rhino. They have a prehensile lip, allowing them mainly to browse on trees, shrubs, legumes and tree seedling rather than grazing. They need to drink at least once a day, and are usually limited to a range within about 5km (3 miles) of water.

Black rhino start to breed at 4-5 years, after which females generally have a calf every two to three years. Calves remain with their mother for several years, so it is normal often to see a female with calves of different ages.

Rhino in the Masai Mara

The Masai Mara is the principal area in Kenya with a population of free-ranging, unfenced wild black rhino. Most large populations, such as at Lewa and Ngulia (Tsavo West) are now in protected, fenced areas.

At present there are 20-25 black rhino in the National Reserve, with 10 in the Mara Triangle, with the rest east of the Mara River, some of them moving between Kenya and the Serengeti, so precise numbers are difficult. The Masai Mara's rhino are given a great deal of attention, with constant monitoring to deter poaching.

A group of black rhino in the balanites savanna

The threat to Rhino

The rhino is the most threatened large mammal on the planet, and at present rates of slaughter will become extinct in the near future.

It is the rhino's horn which makes it so vulnerable, caused by the mistaken and totally unscientific belief that rhino horn has medicinal properties. The demand comes from the Far East, especially China and Vietnam. There the rhino horn, which is very similar to human finger nails, is ground up and used to "cure" all manner of things. The current market price is about $65,000 per kg.

A serious issue, which has limited the areas suitable for rhino recently, has been uncontrolled burning which has taken place annually along the edges of the Reserve, so decimating the browsing habitat. In addition, uncontrolled incursions of cattle have also created a habitat which rhino prefer to avoid.

Black rhino mother and calf

Well hidden in the long grasses

Watching Rhino

Firstly, be aware that you may not always be able to spot rhino, even if they are present in the area. They are mostly active at night. During the day, they prefer to find shade and to sleep. Early morning and dusk are the best times to spot them. And appreciate that being close to a rhino is an enormous privilege.

Be careful not to cause them any stress, especially by driving too close, or by making a lot of noise. Rhino have very poor eye-sight, but their other senses are well-developed. Noise will simply upset the animal.

Be especially sensitive when there is a calf. Rhino are good mothers, and they are aware that the only time their calf is vulnerable is when it is small. So don't get too close. Use your long lens to good effect.

The Future

The future seems bleak. Although overall in East Africa, there has been a steady increase in rhino numbers in recent years, poaching appears to be on the increase, fuelled by the massive hike in the value of rhino horn, influenced no doubt, by the acceleration of wealth in China and southeast Asia. March 2014 saw the first rhino killed in the Mara for some years. Will ours be the last generation to experience rhino in the wild?

Birds

Without doubt, the Masai Mara is one of Africa's best places for watching birds. There are over 500 recorded species, and the area is important for many migrants, as well as resident species.

With so many species, this guide will not try to be comprehensive, but will concentrate on some of the birds which most visitors are likely to see.

If you are particularly interested in birdwatching, it is important to carry a field guide such as "Birds of Kenya and Northern Tanzania" by Zimmerman, Turner and Pearson, along with your binoculars.

The species we shall cover will be some of those which you have a good chance of seeing on an average safari.

We shall look specifically at birds found on the open plain, birds associated with wetlands and water, and finally, the vultures which are major scavengers.

Birds of the plain and the savanna

You are pretty well guaranteed to see what many regard as Kenya's most beautiful bird, the **Lilac-breasted roller** *(Coracias caudatus)*. Often seen perched on a tree-stump looking out for grasshoppers, it is incredibly photogenic, usually giving you plenty of time for a series of photos, before flying off to the next bush or tree-stump.

Lilac-breasted roller, surely Africa's most beautiful bird

The **ground hornbill** (*Ducorvus leadbeaten*) is both spectacular and fairly common and is often found in large groups, strutting around in its search for small reptiles and amphibians.

Ostriches (*Struthio camelus*) are less numerous than in the past, but are still common. The usual sighting is of a small group, including one male bird (much darker than the females) and a group of females, dominated by a "major hen". Ostriches have a social life unlike any other birds, which involves the cock bird and the major hen assuming responsibility for incubation and defence of all the eggs of the group. Ostrich chicks are then often corralled in large nursery groups, looked after by unrelated adult birds.

Some birds seem to be everywhere, and the **Crowned plover** (*Vanellus coronatus*), usually in pairs, is one of these.

Chattering and with spectacular plumage, **Helmeted guinea-fowl** (*Numida meleagris*) are common, as are **Black-bellied bustards.** (*Eupoditis melanogaster*)

The **Secretary bird**, (*Sagittarious serpentarious*) struts around the grasslands, "pens" behind his ear, like a 19th century secretary, hunting for snakes and lizards.

Ground hornbill

Helmeted guinea fowl

Group of ostriches

Crowned plover

African wattled plover

Spur-winged plover

Secretary bird

Black-bellied bustard

Birds of the wetlands

Water and the high water-table left after the rains in some areas of the Triangle result in a whole range of cranes, storks and smaller waterbirds.

The Saddle-billed stork *(Ephippiorhynchus senegalensis)* is large, spectacular and quite common. It feeds on frogs, fish, reptiles and even small birds.

One of the most beautiful birds you will see is the **Crowned crane,** *(Balearica regulorum)* almost always seen in pairs. Their food is wide ranging, from grass seeds and grasshoppers to amphibians, small reptiles and fish. So you will see them in the grasslands as well as in various wetlands.

The Jacana *(Actophilornis africanus)* is found actually in the wetland, walking on its wide, semi-webbed feet across the lily-pads. Jacanas mostly eat insects and invertebrates.

Crowned cranes

Black-headed heron

The Jacana walks across the weeds

The Saddle-billed stork is one of the largest of the wetland birds.

Yellow-billed stork

Apart from a few permanent wet areas, the Triangle wetlands are seasonal, often "lakes" during the rains, but drying out to become lush pastures during the dry seasons. As the habitat changes seasonally, so will the usage by the bird life.

During the period September to about April, the Masai Mara is full of winter migrants from Europe and Asia. These include species such as the **Wood sandpiper**, the **Northern wheatear**, and many of the herons and storks.

Some birds indulge in irregular migration, largely within Africa, dependent mainly on availability of water.

One of these is the **Yellow-billed stork** *(Mycteria ibis)*, which requires wetlands and open water for feeding, and may temporarily leave the Mara during periods of drought.

The **Hamerkop** (*Scopus u. umbretta)* builds an enormous nest

Wood sandpiper

Grey-headed kingfisher

How to identify different vultures

Lappet-faced vulture *(Torgos tracheliotos)*
Very large bird.
Pink head, fleshy "lappets" either side of face. Huge, powerful greyish bill; brown eyes.
Dominates at the kill.

Ruppell's griffon vulture *(Gyps rueppellii)*
Large; similar to White-backed vulture, but has long, yellowish horn bill; white edges to body feathers and upper wing coverts. Yellow/amber eyes; scaly pattern on wings.

African white-backed vulture
(Gyps africanus)
Medium size; smaller than Ruppell's vulture.
Very broad wings; short tail; white neck ruff.
White back patch visible when wings spread.
Juveniles don't have light-coloured back.

White-headed vulture
(Trigonoceps occipitalis)
Small; white head and crop patch.
Bright pink-red bill, with blackish tip.

Hooded vulture
(Necrosyrtes monachus pileatus)
Compact.
Dark brown; slender hooked bill.
Adults have largely bare pink head and neck, feathered at back of head.

Marabou stork
(Leptoptilos crumeniferus)
Also present at most kills.

The importance of vultures.

We all have our own views on vultures.
Maybe we appreciate them as the savanna's most graceful thermal soarers, or perhaps our image is of the squabbling and blood-covered flock which has descended on a kill. Whichever it may be, vultures are hugely important as the garbage collectors of the Mara ecosystem. More than 70% of all meat is believed to be recycled by vultures, so it is vital that their numbers remain healthy. Imagine the thousands of wildebeest carcasses each year, rotting in the Mara River, without the vultures to clean up.

The Threat to Vultures

Recent research shows vultures hugely under threat. Numbers have declined by about 50% in the last 30 years, and the Egyptian vulture, once common, is now locally extinct in the Masai Mara. Poisoning, deliberate or accidental, continues to be a major issue, with the pesticide *carbofuran* responsible for many of the deaths.
It is believed that this may also be the cause of numerous lion deaths each year.

White-backed vultures at a kill with a large lappet-faced vulture to the right

Raptors

In addition to the vultures, the Mara boasts about 50 raptors, and is one of the best places in Africa to see a wide range of eagles, falcons, harriers and hawks. You will see them in the sky, roosting on all manner of trees, and attendant at a kill. Sadly this guide simply cannot cope with the numbers of different bird species, and so we suggest you invest in a good bird book which will cover all the species. A complete checklist is also available on:
www.maratriangle.org/maratriangle/bird-list

Tawny eagle

How to improve your wildlife watching

> **Big 5 or bust?**
> There is no one way to watch wildlife. However, many visitors spend their time on safari almost in a panic to tick all the boxes. Big 5 or bust! There are better ways. These are some suggestions.

Big five or bust!

Think about the seasons.
This most likely means being aware of the phases of the migrations. Do you want to see hundreds of thousands of wildebeest and zebra (and the tourist high season), or do you want to come at a quieter, more peaceful time?
July to October give you the migrations, but other times still have thousands of animals and fewer visitors.

> **Bring a pair of good binoculars.**
> You will see so much more. Light-weight binoculars are more comfortable to use all day than higher powered heavy-weights.
> Make sure your camera has a reasonable zoom lens, minimum 300 mm. Most camps and lodges have recharging facilities.

Find out as much as you can about the animals you wish to see.
For example, lion sleep most of the day and become more lively as dusk approaches, so 4.00 pm onwards will be a more productive time to look for lion, or in the morning, perhaps after a night of hunting, and gorging themselves on a kill.

> **Think "water"**
> Almost all animals need to drink, usually once a day. So rivers and pools are usually the best places to guarantee seeing wildlife. In addition, predators such as lion and leopard use this fact in their hunting, and many kills are made close to water-holes and rivers.

Try staying in one place.
Decide on a spot, and to stay there for an hour or so. It might be a small watering place, a stretch of river, or a crossing point. Maybe the edge of a piece of woodland. You will be surprised at what you see.

Try the more remote areas of the Triangle.
Explore further south along the Mara River, or in the southwest towards Ngiro-are, along the Tanzanian border, or along the Escarpment. In these places there may be just as many animals, and many fewer visitors.

Look for some of the Masai Mara's over 500 recorded bird species.
One cannot miss some of the larger birds such as Crowned cranes, or Saddle-billed storks, but many of the species are found in bush or woodland. So you need to stop, wait and use your binoculars and your camera to best effect. Come with a good bird book. See page 54.

Know where you are.
Follow the map in the front of this guidebook.

At the border between Kenya and Tanzania

Finally, take an interest in the little things.
Look for small mammals like mongoose, of which the Triangle has several species, tortoises such as the Leopard tortoise, fifth largest in the world, butterflies, dung beetles, flowers, and the wonderfully coloured Agama lizard.

Some of the "little things"

Dung beetle

Eurasian bee-eater

Leopard tortoise

Large striped swallowtail butterfly

Agama lizard

Waterlily

Dwarf mongoose

61

The enjoyment of visitors and the sustainability of the Reserve depend on visitors following a series of simple rules and guidelines. This ensures least disturbance to wildlife, and optimises the visitor experience. Here is an extract from the rules of the Mara Triangle:

MARA TRIANGLE PARK RULES

Please keep to the speed limits: 50 km/hr on graded roads, 30 km/hr all others.

Always slow down for animals.

Do not drive off-road in High Use & River Zones. There are signs to help you.

Keep to graded roads and cut tracks in above zones.

Off-roading in Low Use Zone is allowed to view big cats.

Always stay more than 25 metres away from the animals.

Please, no shouting, clapping or cheering.

Do not sit nor stand on vehicle's roof at any time.

No more than 5 vehicles at wildlife sightings. *

No alighting from vehicles at river crossing points.

Do not cross Tanzanian border.

Do not chase, follow or harass animals.

No littering.

Leave park or be in camp/lodge by 7:00pm.

* When there are more than five vehicles waiting to see an animal, viewing time is restricted to 10 minutes. Vehicles waiting to see the sighting must wait at a distance of 100 metres. Please respect the rules and our rangers, who are there to ensure the protection of the wildlife and the environment.

The two most problematic issues are off-road driving and having too many vehicles at an animal sighting, especially during river crossings. Clearly this is an area where you, the visitor, can help. If you are the driver, we simply ask you to follow the rules. If your driver breaks the rules, you can politely ask him to stick to the rules.

This is unacceptable

If you break any of these rules, rangers have the legal right to:
Impose an on-the-spot fine of KSh 10,000.
Have a vehicle and/or people removed from the park immediately.
Have a vehicle and/or people banned from the park.

Other Guidelines
In addition to the rules:
No lighting of fires
No feeding of animals
No collecting of trophies, such as bones, shells, geological specimens, plants etc.

Photographing people
Many people are sensitive to being photographed, so in general ask their permission first. Do not be surprised if you are asked to pay a fee for your images.

GAME DRIVES

What is a game drive?

The idea of the game drive is that you drive out, usually early in the morning at day-break, or in the last two or three hours of the day, when animals are most active. As you will note from various sections of this guide, animal locations are not random. Both prey and predators will be where they are for a reason. On the game drive you try to locate them.

For each drive, a route is shown on a section of the map with suggestions as to what you might see. During the annual migrations, you will see huge herds of wildebeest and zebra more or less everywhere.

1. River Road

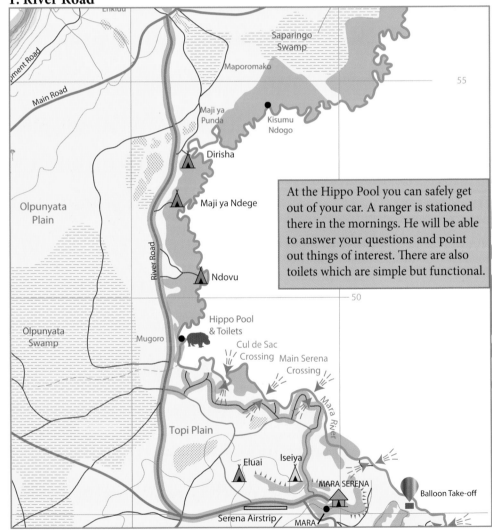

At the Hippo Pool you can safely get out of your car. A ranger is stationed there in the mornings. He will be able to answer your questions and point out things of interest. There are also toilets which are simple but functional.

A group of female waterbuck resting

Nile crocodiles basking on a sandbank

River Road

Whether you approach from the north or the south, this little section along the Mara river generally gives you the best chance of seeing the widest range of animals, on almost any day of the year.

Either side of the Hippo Pool, you will usually see a variety of antelope and gazelle, including topi, waterbuck, impala, also Thomson's gazelle, and loads of scampering warthog.

You may be lucky to come across a lion kill by the Mogoro pride from the previous night, and spotted hyena skulking home to their den to sleep. South of the Hippo Pool there are several good places for spotting large numbers of the Mara river's big Nile crocodiles, sunning themselves on a sandbank .

There are hippo pods all along the river. In the early morning, look out for lone hippos returning to the river after a night's grazing.

This is a good place to spot elephant families in their daily march to their favoured drinking spot on the river.

A family of elephant leaving the river

2. The Inselbergs

The inselbergs are small, flat-topped hills, located in the south of the Triangle with a special charm of their own (see page 23).

Heading southwest, start along the track which leaves the main road just south of the Ngiro-are junction. In the dry season, the swamp to your right will be dry, but you will notice a swathe of darker green, well-watered grass, which is favoured by the larger herbivores.

Ahead is a group of inselbergs, and we invite you to be sensitive to the variable landscape. No longer are there flat plains with grass going on forever, but hills, valleys, steep slopes and gentle slopes. There are rocky areas and well-watered valley bottoms.

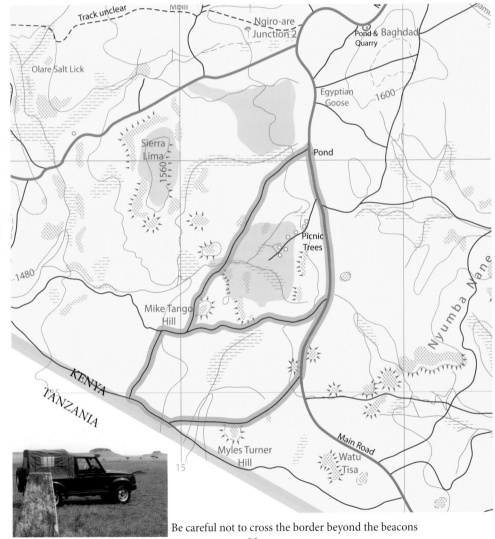

Be careful not to cross the border beyond the beacons

As you drive up to and through the inselbergs, consider the rocky bushland where you might see dik-dik and klipspringer, and impala around the edge of the thicket. Lower down will be the larger grazing animals, such as zebra, topi and eland. If there are elephant and buffalo, they most likely will prefer the better-watered valley bottoms.

Keep your eyes open for lion sheltering in a thicket from the heat of the sun. This is the core area of the Egyptian Goose pride. They will most likely see you. Will you be lucky enough to see them?

You can continue right down to the Tanzania border, shown on the ground with large concrete beacons. Use your map, and make sure you do not cross into Tanzania illegally. Here you will get the feeling of being in Serengeti, "plains which go on forever".

Return by the Main Road.

Think like an animal.
"Where are the rocky places?
Where is the short grass? Where is the juicy, well watered grass? Where is it safe?
Where is the leopard?
Where can I browse?
Where can I keep a good lookout?"

Long grass hides many dangers

3. The Escarpment Road

Start in the south from the track which leaves near Fig Tree on the main Ngiro-are road, west of the Olpunyata swamp. The road goes north between the Maasai cattle trails (See page 6), until at the foot of the escarpment it turns right.

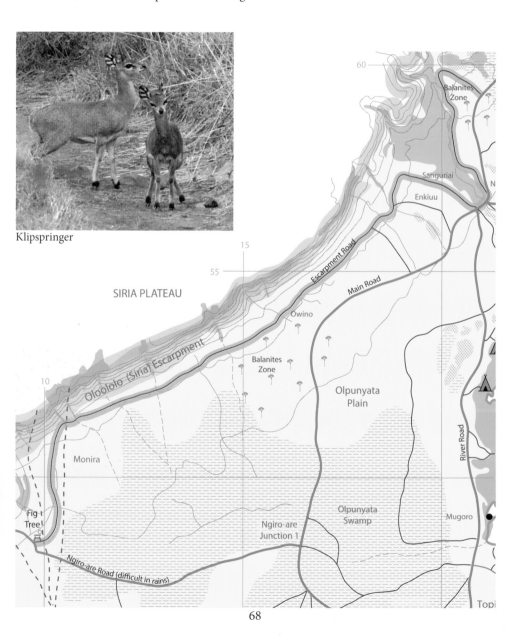

Klipspringer

The Oloololo Escarpment is a whole wildlife experience on its own, but is relatively inaccessible. However, the fairly recently made Escarpment Road allows the best access.

Refer to the Habitats section, page 22. You will see that the escarpment probably has more variety than any other part of the Triangle, with landscapes ranging from rocky crags, boulder strewn slopes, to well-watered wetlands. So you are likely to see almost anything, and with very few or no other vehicles around. And some superb views.

This is the core area of the Sausage Tree pride of lions.

At the far end of the drive, you may wish to continue beyond the Sanguraia bridge and head back towards the escarpment to the idyllic location named Out of Africa. See Picnic Sundowner spots, pages 80-81.

Northern escarpment

GAME DRIVES

4. The far southwest and the border track

If you have a whole day, take a packed lunch and make for
the southwest corner of the Triangle, and then head down
along the border. As this is a fairly remote area, where you
may not see another vehicle, take a ranger and make sure
you have a working radio.
Also, take plenty of food and water in case you get stuck.

N

SIRIA PLATEAU

Owino

Balanites
Zone

Olpunyata
Plain

Monira

Fig
Tree

Ngiro-are
Junction 1

Olpunyata
Swamp

Mugoro

Mawe ya Sang
(Sang's rock)

Kishanga

Cattle Trail

Acacia Woods

Entikin

START

Ngiro-are
Outpost

Ilijito

Fig Tree

Balanites
Zone

Kopa & Baghdad
Quarry

Ngiro-are
Swamp

Nyah
One

Track unclear

Mulima
Mbili

Ngiro-are
Junction 2

Olare Salt Lick

Egyptian
Goose

Endoinyo
Olpaek

Olare Road

Sierra
Lima

Pond

Endoinyo
Nasipa

Picnic
Trees

Army
Drift

Mike Tango
Hill

Myles Turner
Hill

Main Road

Watu

70

The drive follows the Ngiro-are road across the swamp, past the Fig Tree, across the Maasai Cattle trails and along the foot of the escarpment. Huge granite boulders have plunged down from the crags above, creating habitat for the creatures which love rocky places.

The streams which flow down the face of the escarpment generally never make it to the valley floor, but percolate into the slope, to re-emerge lower down, south of the road. Here they create the wetlands much loved by large herds of elephant.

Soon the landscape changes, and you are in beautiful acacia savanna, with grassland which is punctuated by scattered Acacia gerrardii. There are elephant, impala and other herbivores. This is one of the loveliest habitats in the Triangle and well worth spending time here.

With the Ngiro-are outpost in sight, the drive then turns off the road to a track to the left, (southeast along the border). After crossing the Ngiro-are river, just a trickle in the dry season, the track may go through an area which is very wet, depending on the season, so take advice from your ranger. The track may well be flooded.

From here towards Purungat bridge is the longest track in the Mara Triangle, and one which will give you that real "Serengeti" experience. In Maasai "Serengeti" means "endless plains", plains which go on seemingly forever. Being out in this sort of landscape is almost a spiritual experience, and so let it wash over you.

Depending on the season, you will see all sorts of plains animals here. You will also pass through the core area of the Border pride of lion, so you may happen to come across them. Don't forget to pay attention to areas of thicket for lion lying up during the heat of the day.

Acacia savanna at the foot of the escarpment

5. Rhino spotting

You have a good chance of seeing rhino in the Triangle, especially if you seek the advice of rangers on the most recent sightings. However, this game drive will put you in the general area where you will most likely find them.

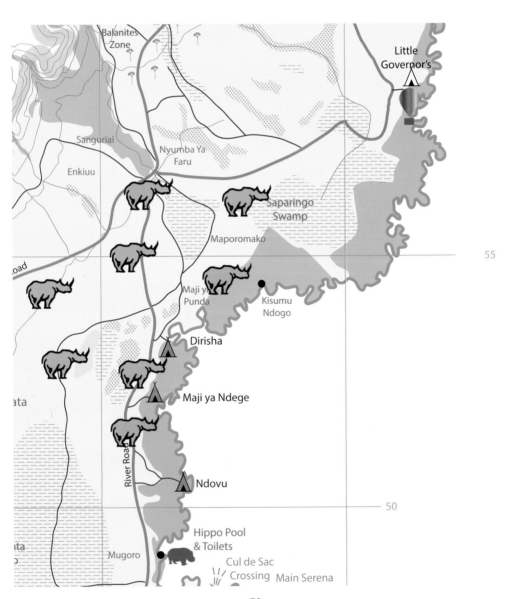

It is helpful to consider the rhino's usual daily cycle. Firstly, Black rhino often spend much of the day sleeping in shade, so early morning and just before dark are the most likely times to see them.

Although they are browsers rather than grass-eaters, Black rhino in the Triangle also favour the low shrubs and herbs growing in the Olpunyata Swamp area.

So the most likely rhino spotting location is along the edge of the riverine woodland, anywhere from about Ndovu campsite northwards. And when you are looking for rhino, take time with your binoculars. Although they are big animals, you may have to patiently search them out, either coming back to the woods, or setting off in the morning.

Oxpecker and Ruppell's starling

Joseph Kimojino, senior warden

Sleeping giants

6. Elephant in the "Swamp"

There are probably more elephant in the Mara Triangle at the moment than for many years. One habitat where they congregate during the dry season, at least until the wildebeest arrive, is in those areas shown with a marsh symbol on the map. These places are flooded in the rains, and remain with a high water-table and lush grass, when the rains have stopped.

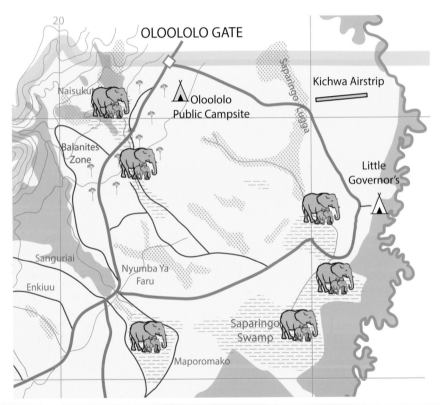

A high water-table creates lush grass

There are many of these wetlands in the northern Triangle between the escarpment and the Mara river south of Little Governors' camp. As you scan out across the plains, the seasonal marshes show up as darker green areas of still-growing grasses. These are the zones into which the streams from the escarpment disappear, maintaining a high water-table. Elephant love these areas with their juicy grass, and it is common to see lots of family groups of maybe 12 -15 animals, with some females, lots of calves of different ages, and occasionally a bull looking to mate with a female in season.

Elephant life stages mirror the pattern in people.

GAME DRIVES

Maasai Saturday at Olare
Every two weeks, on a Saturday morning, the Maasai herders from the top of the Oloololo Escarpment exercise a traditional right, and bring their herds to drink at the Olare Salt-lick springs in the southern Mara Triangle. From before dawn, perhaps 3000 cattle, sheep and goats stream down the well-worn trails at the head of the Ngiro-are river, trekking about 12 km into the Triangle to drink at the salt springs and graze for a few hours.

As we explain in the section on the Maasai, the Masai Mara exists and only continues to be sustainable because of the Maasai people. In your camp or lodge, you will encounter highly bedecked Maasai who come to dance and sell trinkets. Those herding their animals to the Salt lick are not "tourist Maasai". The most they might ask is if you have any water. So it is a good idea to take some spare bottles with you.

Start early, and we suggest you take the route along the Ngiro-are road through the swamp towards the escarpment, to see the swarms of animals coming down into the Triangle.
Stop, switch off your engine, and listen to the distinctive, unforgettable sound of cowbells and the yodel-like singing of the herders. Maasai described in the Bible, Chronicles chapter 1, were named as "singers". Enjoy the peace. Most likely yours will be the only vehicle.

Then continue towards the anti-poaching outpost, turning left (south), doing some careful map-reading, before turning left (east), after a bulge in the road, in a broad, shallow valley, with the stream outlined by scattered trees, towards the head of Olare where you will begin to pick up watering and grazing cattle.
Return by the same track or continue east towards the main road.
Enjoy the tranquillity, the cow-bells and the Maasai singing.

Below: Streams of cattle head towards Olare salt-lick

7. Maasai Saturday

8. Balloon Safari

For many visitors, a balloon safari over the Masai Mara is one of those experiences of a lifetime. There is simply nothing quite like floating over the plains of the Mara, the sun just rising, and the herds spread out below.
Silent except for the occasional short bursts of the burners creating fresh hot air, the balloon drifts along, part of the ever-so-gentle breeze.

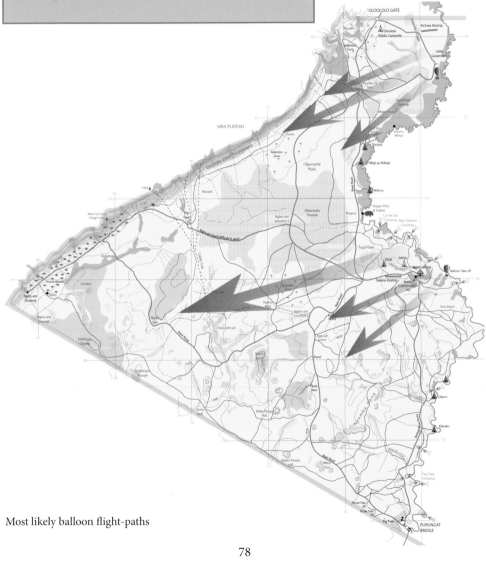

Most likely balloon flight-paths

Each balloon trip starts just before dawn, with an early morning call and hot tea or coffee. When you arrive at the take-off site, the balloon is already partly inflated. The wicker basket takes about 16 people, and at sunrise, with a final blast of hot air from the burners, the balloon gently lifts off, and as it slowly gains height, usually drifts towards the southwest. Below, depending on the time of year, there are thousands of wildebeest and zebra, herds of elephant and buffalo, and perhaps a pride of lion, finishing their kill of the previous night. With your vantage point, you could see almost anything.

The trip usually lasts for about 40 minutes, with the direction and landing zone controlled by the breeze. Landing can be interesting, depending on whether there is much of a wind. The pilot will put the basket down on grassland, but he has little control of exactly where. Sometimes it can be like the landing of a feather; at others it may be a bit bumpy, with the basket dragged along a short distance, until it stops.

Balloon take-off at dawn

View into the balloon canopy

By the time you disembark from your balloon, breakfast will already have been assembled nearby. The full works, tables with linen cloths, and, just what you need at 8.00 in the morning, champagne to celebrate your epic journey.

The flights are usually booked before dinner the evening before. Balloons in the Triangle fly from two sites, one at Serena and one at Little Governors'.

9. Picnics & Sundowners

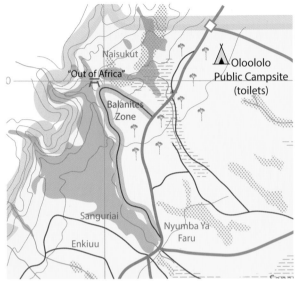

Picnics and Sundowners

There is a fine tradition in Kenya of alfresco dining and drinking in beautiful places. If you have seen the film "Out of Africa" you will have the right idea.

Often located beside a tree for some shade, it's especially enjoyable if there is also a nice view.

Waterbuck enjoy the picnic spot too

Out of Africa

This is a special spot, tucked under the escarpment, in the northern Triangle.

Drive on the track north of the Sanguraia river and forest. As you gain height near the escarpment, you will eventually arrive at a little knoll, surmounted by a balanite tree, and with the most beautiful view over the northern Triangle. This is just the place for your sundowner, and for thinking those special thoughts, as you muse about this amazing place. Those in the Mara Triangle call this spot "Out of Africa".

There are numerous designated "picnic trees" in the Triangle, and we will mention those and a few more.

Purungat Bridge

The Purungat Bridge is an area where visitors may get out of their cars, see the hippos in the Mara river, use the toilets, and have a picnic. This is also where you can buy a map, an atlas or a guidebook.

Hippo pool near Purungat Bridge

Picnic Trees

There are several locations designated "picnic trees" just to the south or west of the Main road. Refer to the map. There are no facilities other than a lovely place to have your picnic.

The Hippo Pool

There are scores of hippo pools, but the one north of Serena is special, has a nice view, a ranger to answer questions, and that other essential, toilets.

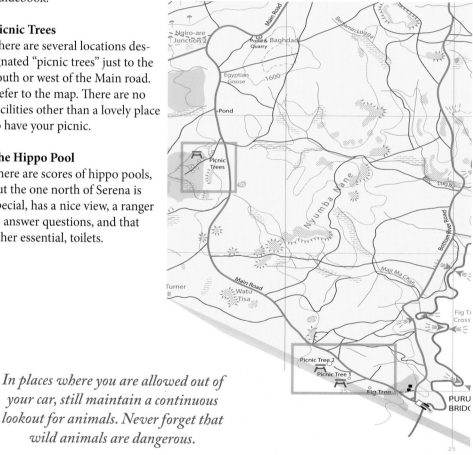

In places where you are allowed out of your car, still maintain a continuous lookout for animals. Never forget that wild animals are dangerous.

A Wonder of the Natural World

No-one can fail to be moved by the Great Migration, the world's greatest year-round movement of large mammals. It involves about 2 million animals, which, annually for thousands of years, have trekked around the ecosystem of Serengeti and Masai Mara, motivated by differences in soils and rainfall, in search of grazing.

About 1.5 million wildebeest take part, along with 200,000 zebra, 350,000 Thomson's gazelle, and a few thousand eland.

When did the world know?

In the 1950s the father and son team, Bernard and Michael Grzimek, began to count the wildebeest in Serengeti. They were both zoologists from Frankfurt Zoological Society. Using a small aeroplane, they made the first attempts to evaluate the enormity of the migrations. In 1959 they published the book "Serengeti Shall Not Die", thus bringing the attention of the world to this amazing phenomenon.

Sadly, Michael died while doing this work, when his aircraft collided with a vulture in southeast Serengeti.

Why does the migration occur?

Over many thousands of years, just as birds seasonally migrate all over the world, so do wildebeest and zebra move around the Serengeti ecosystem. Whether or not each animal rationalises its movement is doubtful, though some believe so. But the benefits from the variations in rainfall and soils between southern Serengeti and the Masai Mara are clear, with each complementing the other. At different times of year, the wildebeest need to be in what they perceive to be "the right place".

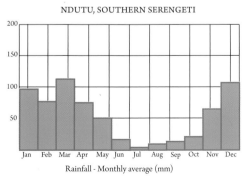

NDUTU, SOUTHERN SERENGETI

Rainfall - Monthly average (mm)

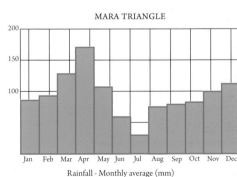

MARA TRIANGLE

Rainfall - Monthly average (mm)

Left: Wildebeest begin to move north from the calving grounds

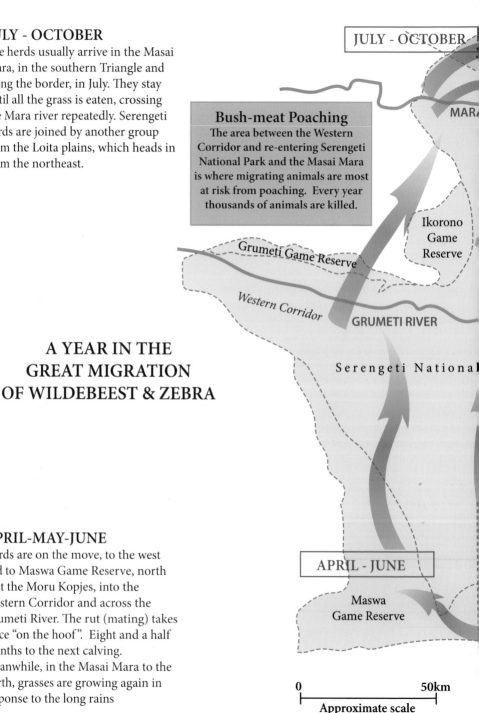

JULY - OCTOBER
The herds usually arrive in the Masai Mara, in the southern Triangle and along the border, in July. They stay until all the grass is eaten, crossing the Mara river repeatedly. Serengeti herds are joined by another group from the Loita plains, which heads in from the northeast.

Bush-meat Poaching
The area between the Western Corridor and re-entering Serengeti National Park and the Masai Mara is where migrating animals are most at risk from poaching. Every year thousands of animals are killed.

JULY - OCTOBER

MARA

Ikorono Game Reserve

Grumeti Game Reserve

Western Corridor

GRUMETI RIVER

Serengeti National

A YEAR IN THE GREAT MIGRATION OF WILDEBEEST & ZEBRA

APRIL-MAY-JUNE
Herds are on the move, to the west and to Maswa Game Reserve, north past the Moru Kopjes, into the Western Corridor and across the Grumeti River. The rut (mating) takes place "on the hoof". Eight and a half months to the next calving. Meanwhile, in the Masai Mara to the north, grasses are growing again in response to the long rains

APRIL - JUNE

Maswa Game Reserve

0   50km
Approximate scale

84

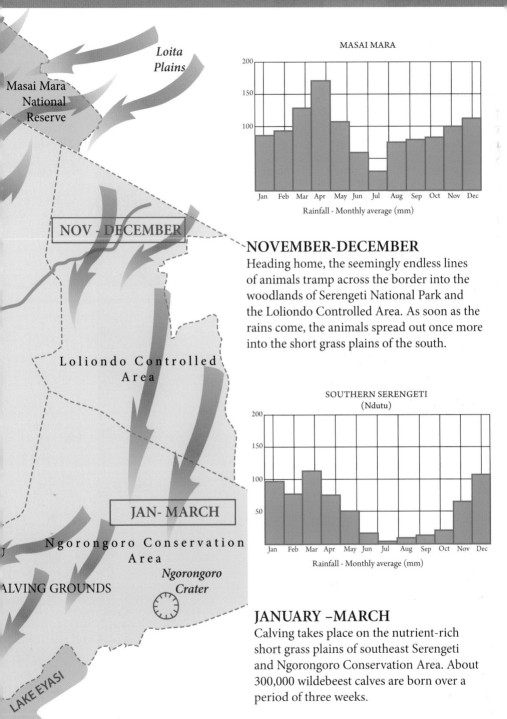

Loita Plains

Masai Mara National Reserve

MASAI MARA

Rainfall - Monthly average (mm)

NOV - DECEMBER

NOVEMBER-DECEMBER

Heading home, the seemingly endless lines of animals tramp across the border into the woodlands of Serengeti National Park and the Loliondo Controlled Area. As soon as the rains come, the animals spread out once more into the short grass plains of the south.

Loliondo Controlled Area

SOUTHERN SERENGETI
(Ndutu)

Rainfall - Monthly average (mm)

JAN- MARCH

Ngorongoro Conservation Area

Ngorongoro Crater

ALVING GROUNDS

JANUARY –MARCH

Calving takes place on the nutrient-rich short grass plains of southeast Serengeti and Ngorongoro Conservation Area. About 300,000 wildebeest calves are born over a period of three weeks.

LAKE EYASI

River crossing

The Main C

The Crossing of the Mara River

By the time the wildebeest arrive, the Mara River is a languid stream, between 20 and 50 metres wide. But its apparent peace belies its dangers, and annually thousands of animals will die attempting to cross it. There are not only Africa's biggest crocodiles lying in wait, but jagged rocks to snare terrified animals, and sheer banks frequently making escape from the river almost impossible, and lastly the sheer panic of thousands of animals trying to cross the river all at once.

To get to the southern Triangle, the migration route will already have crossed the combined Mara-Sand River. So the animals already know the dangers of a river crossing.

Wildebeest and zebra often congregate in their thousands on the banks of the river prior to crossing, almost waiting for the signs to be right. They mainly use long-established crossing points, so we generally know where crossings will be. The massing of the herd may go on for hours, then one brave animal will step into the water, and the rest, perhaps 10,000 will follow, frequently in the most frenzied activity seen in the animal world.

Wildebeest and zebra waiting for the right time

In a good crossing only a few will be taken by crocodiles. However, huge numbers of animals often fail to arrive at the gently, shelving exit point on the opposite bank, and end up too far downstream, to be met with the sheer, earthen banks found along most of the river.

Panic ensues, and wildebeest upon wildebeest try to escape from the water, and large numbers can die. However the vast majority successfully make the crossing, often only to repeat it a few days later.

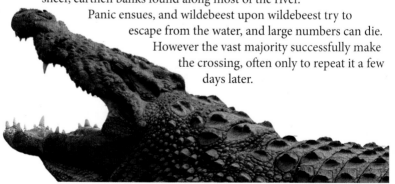

THE MAASAI

The Maasai and the Mara

Unlike a national park which, in Kenya, is owned by the nation, the Masai Mara is a national "reserve", and is owned by the Maasai people. Furthermore, it exists in all its richness, largely because of the way, for the last 300 years, these people have inter-acted with the wildlife in a sustainable rather than a destructive way.

"Masai" and "Maasai"?

The "Maasai" are the people who speak the language "Maa". So technically all spellings of the name should have a double "aa". However, over time, especially with regard to the name of the National Reserve, use of a single "a", eg"Masai" has crept in, and is commonly used. With regard to the Maasai people, the double "aa" should always be used.

Left: Maasai grandmother with her grandchild

Maasai men spend much of their time in conversation

88

Who are the Maasai?

The Maasai are certainly East Africa's most famous tribe, and the one, which fascinates the visitor above all others.

There are many reasons for this, especially the distinctive red-ochre "shukas" (blankets or cloaks) worn by the spear-carrying men, and the mass of bangles and beads of the women. The Maasai are handsome people, sometimes seen as aloof, almost arrogant.

Their lives revolve around cattle, and many still live in their traditional housing.

However, above all, they are people who have most resisted change, and who have generally refused to adopt the western way of life. They are their own people.

Maasai life revolves around cattle

Maasai men playing the board game *enkeshui*

History

Maasai oral history goes back about 300 years, and recounts an earlier home in present-day Sudan, in the Nile Valley. Movement southwards was clearly a gradual process, rather than a sudden invasion, and it has given rise to two identifiable groups.

These are the Northern Maasai including the Samburu and Chamu, and secondly the Southern Maasai of southern Kenya and northern Tanzania. In recent years, modern genetic and linguistic research have given us clues, stretching the story back over thousands of years. The Maasai have genetic links with other groups in northern Africa, and potential connections with Holy Land in the eastern Mediterranean. The name "Maasai" appears in chapter 9 in the book of 1 Chronicles of the Bible, and the names Korah and Kore, which relate to the Samburu, also appear in Chronicles and in Numbers. Ecologist and Maa speaker, Mike Rainy, reminds us that the Maasai pray "Nkai ai Oi Pasinai", meaning "My God, given at Sinai". So it would seem that there may be a connection between the Maasai and the Jews.

Photograph taken by the author in 1964

Rinderpest killed 95% of all the cattle in the 1890s

"Emutai" - the decade of disaster

The modern history of the Maasai begins at the end of the nineteenth century. By the end of the 1880s, although the Maasai only numbered about 100,000, they occupied about 60% of what is modern-day Kenya. Although ferocious warriors, the dominance of the Maasai had a powerful protective influence, insulating their more sedentary neighbours from the ravages of slavery which affected the coastal region and lands around them in East Africa.
1893 saw the start of a decade of disaster, the period the Maasai call "Emutai".
European colonisation brought with it death and disease. Rinderpest killed approximately 95% of all the cattle on which the Maasai depended, and also many of the wild animals such as buffalo and wildebeest.
Smallpox and cholera did the same to the people, with about 60% of the population dying during that decade. To add misery to misery, the years 1897 and 1898 saw the worst droughts in a generation, killing many of the few cattle which were left.
Recovery came with the vaccination of cattle, and the eradication of rinderpest.
For the people, modern medicine, establishment of clinics and the control or eradication of human diseases such as smallpox, brought recovery. The present Southern population of Maasai, between Kenya and Tanzania is now about 1 million.

THE MAASAI

Cattle are the major sign of wealth

The Role of Cattle

Maasai life is centred on cattle, and it is likely that the ability of both cattle and their herders to move according to the seasons, has been the basis of their survival.

Homes are located around the "enkang" or "manyatta". Animals are kept within a thorn stockade at night. Cattle are the major sign of wealth, and a medium of exchange. Products of cattle, milk, blood, hides and even dung (for house building and as a fuel), are all central to the way of life.

Unlike other tribes, Maasai have never had a tradition of hunting wild animals for food, but depend on their cows, together with sheep and goats. Effectively they live at peace with the wildlife.

When drought comes, they have the ability to migrate to wherever there is pasture, occasionally even to parks in Nairobi.

Maasai also depend on sheep and goats for food

Maasai and the Reserve

There are still traditional pastoralists above the Oloololo Escarpment, and to the north of the Triangle, but cattle are not allowed to graze legally within the National Reserve. However, closely managed grazing by cattle is allowed in the conservancies, mainly to clear tall grass, disliked by wildebeest and gazelle, so that it can be replaced by new, short, succulent pastures.

Maasai cattle are allowed into the Triangle on alternate Saturdays, to visit the Olare salt lick and springs, where the cattle drink the mineral rich water. Up to 3000 animals, cattle, sheep and goats pour down the well-worn trails, and spend a time at the water, then grazing, before heading home to the Kilgoris Plateau.

The Maasai today

Maasai life is changing, and for many reasons. Probably most important is the fencing of land, in either individual or group ownership, preventing or limiting the one thing which has made life possible for the Maasai, through good times and bad, the freedom to roam.

In addition, many grazing lands, such as the Masai Mara National Reserve, and new conservancies to the north and east, are no longer freely open for Maasai cattle grazing. Although some are open for managed grazing, in general any income now comes from tourists rather than cattle. The huge expanse of Serengeti to the south, is now also closed to cattle.

Additionally, as almost all Maasai children are now educated, horizons are being widened and some Maasai are moving to the towns, and into other jobs.

Those who stay with their traditional life increasingly need to take part in the monetary system, for school fees and uniforms, for cattle vaccinations, and increasingly for their own transport, often starting with a motor-bike.

The Future

Ecologist Mike Rainy, who has lived and worked with the Samburu and the Southern Maasai most of his working life, is optimistic about the future.

"Make no mistake, modern young Maa-speaking men and women are as much part of this new information age as anyone else, and they will surprise themselves and the rest of us by tapping their very deep, life-tolerant, cultural roots, coming up with new solutions to what may appear to be impossible conservation problems.

Let's not imagine that the Maasai are now at a cultural and conservation dead-end".

Perhaps some of us struggle to be so optimistic. Let us hope Mike Rainy is right.

Above and left: Maasai dancing at a cultural boma

Conservation and management

Since 2001, the Mara Triangle has been managed by the not-for-profit management company, Mara Conservancy. The model now established is seen as one of the most effective in East Africa, a total transformation from that existing at the end of the 1990s.

When Mara Conservancy took over, there was not a single operational vehicle. Revenue collection was about 20% of its potential, poaching was out of control, and many roads were unusable. Inevitably, staff morale was at a low ebb.

Mara Conservancy has transformed the management of this part of the Masai Mara National Reserve. The achievements and hopes for the future are summed up in the Vision Statement.

Purungat Gate

MARA CONSERVANCY
Protecting the Mara Triangle
www.maratriangle.org

Mara Conservancy has some well-maintained , heavy-weight equipment.

Mara Conservancy
VISION STATEMENT

Working with local leaders, communities, and tourism partners, the Mara Conservancy uses effective and efficient management methods that enhance the economical value of conservation to better protect the Mara Triangle and its surrounding ecosystem.

We see the Mara Triangle as an integral part of the Greater Mara Ecosystem, which deserves a healthy environment that benefits both people and wildlife. The Mara Conservancy is committed to helping local communities adopt a sustainable approach to conservation by creating a management model that is transparent, accountable and values wildlife.

We believe in responsible tourism, sustainable development, good guiding practices, and strive for an environment that is free from the theats of poaching. This is achieved by fostering good working relationships with local communities and tourism stakeholders, recognising the worth of an appreciated workforce, and understanding the urgent need to protect our wildlife.

We want to ensure that the Masai Mara remains an important ecosystem for wildlife, tourism, local communities, and for Kenya.

Mara Conservancy achievements so far:

* A clamp down on poaching in the Mara Triangle and the surrounding area.

* Improvement of infrastructure by grading a network of roads within the Triangle, as well as access roads to camps and lodges outside of the Triangle.

* Maintaining a network of secondary roads and tracks to improve wildlife viewing.

* Restoration of existing ranger stations and installation of renewable energy and water harvesting systems.

* Establishment of a transparent and modern (IT based) revenue collection systems.

* Strengthening relationships between the Reserve and the surrounding areas by encouraging community projects and reward schemes for co-habiting with wildlife.

* Encouragement of sound eco-tourism principles among camps and lodges.

The whole of the Masai Mara National Reserve is now under the umbrella of Narok County, which receives 55% of revenue. 36% is retained for conservation & management with the remainder going to KAPS who collect the revenue.

Rangers are on hand at the Hippo Pool

What will visitors see of management and conservation on the ground?

Roads and tracks
Most obvious to the visitor is the road network, which is superbly kept, an excellent advert for Mara Conservancy management of the Mara Triangle.
There isn't a maze of tracks created by indisciplined drivers which is seen in some other areas. In "High Usage areas" where is says "No off-road driving", that is what it means, and almost everyone keeps to this.

Obey the signs placed around the reserve

Low density tourism
Tourism is low density in the Triangle, and Mara Conservancy has resisted the demand for more camps and lodges, leaving only one lodge and one camp actually in the Reserve. This has a major positive benefit for visitors, in that it allows low density tourism, with less crowding of animals than in other areas.

Rhino have returned
The priority given to the anti-poaching measures has meant that the rhino have returned. The northern area of the Mara Triangle is once again a good location to view Black rhino, and there is a small but stable population.

Oloololo Gate

Anti-poaching operation

Rhino have returned to the Triangle

How to get there by air

The quickest and most comfortable way is to fly. Unless you are travelling from another reserve or national park, flights normally begin at Nairobi's Wilson Airport, Kenya's hub for small plane domestic flights. There are no direct flights between the Masai Mara and Serengeti.

The flight to Masai Mara takes from 45 minutes to an hour, depending on which of numerous airstrips you are arriving at. In the Triangle there are two strips, one at Serena, and the other near Kichwa Tembo. Little Governors' guests arrive at Governors' airstrip east of the river, and then cross by ferry.

The main domestic airlines, Safarilink and Airkenya, are based in Nairobi, with Mombasa Air Safari at the coast. Plus there are many other small, charter companies.

www.safarilink.com
www.airkenya.com
www.mombasaairsafaris.com

Think of the flight as part of your safari adventure. Flights from Wilson usually set off over Nairobi National Park, then cross over the Ngong Hills. (Remember *Out of Africa*, both film and book. "I had a farm in Africa, at the foot of the Ngong Hills") You then cross over the Great Rift Valley, with the volcano Suswa to your right, and another volcano, Longanot in the distance. Then over the Loita Plains and into the Greater Masai Mara, usually calling first in the Triangle.

How to get there by road

Alternatively, you can go by road, a journey which takes 4 or 5 hours, usually with a stop in Narok. Travelling by road is a mixed blessing. You certainly get in much closer touch with Kenya, and the journey is spectacular, but Kenyan roads can still be awful, in spite of a general trend towards improvement.

Typical safari vehicles

The usual route from Nairobi starts on the road to Naivasha, plunging down the side of the Great Rift Valley to Mai Mahiu, where you turn left before setting out across the floor of the valley on the road to Narok, the main administrative centre for the Maasai.

Beyond Narok, there are two options. The route through the eastern part of the Reserve turns left at Ewaso Nyiro and goes through Sekenani Gate, about 90 km beyond Narok. This road varies according to maintenance, but is usable in all weathers.

The western route definitely needs 4-wheel drive during and after the rains. After Narok do not head for Ewaso Nyero, but keep on the tarmac road towards Bomet. After about 35 km, turn left towards Nkorkorri, Lemek and Aitong. The section between Aitong and the Mara bridge can be very sticky in the rains, and becomes highly braided.

Another, generally all-weather road via Kilgoris allows access from the west.

See maps pages 4-7.

Where to stay

Since the 1970s, staying in the Triangle has been either in a classical "Out of Africa" safari camp like Little Governors', or at what is now a traditional safari lodge, like Mara Serena. Within the Mara Triangle there are also basic budget campsites, with simple facilities, and also exclusive-use, private campsites, mainly along the river (see maps, pages 4-7)
To the north, outside the National Reserve, there are numerous camps which tend to use the Triangle as their principal area for game drives.

Mara Serena
The lodge is beautifully located in the centre of the Triangle, on a hill, overlooking the Mara river, and the plains of Rhino Ridge and Emarti Hill beyond.

The welcoming new entrance to Mara Serena

The public areas have been recently refurbished, greatly increasing the original lounge and dining areas.
Extra facilities include 24 hour electricity, swimming pool, spa with sauna and gymnasium, wi-fi and also conference centre. Balloon safaris can be booked here, and Serena airstrip is only 5 minutes from the lodge.

Right: Maasai cowbells inspired the design of the lampshades

Accommodation comprises over 70 rooms, taking about 150 guests. Room design is based on the traditional Maasai dwelling, and the interiors are uniquely colourful, with a décor which is echoed throughout the lodge. Bathrooms are en-suite, and every room has a lovely view of the river and the plains.

Accommodation modules are tucked discreetly around the hillside

Food is international, with a wide range of choices, and there is a mixture of buffet and table service.

The design theme continues in the dining area

Left: Mara Serena swimming pool

Little Governors' Camp

Little Governors' is located on the edge of a wetland which occupies a former meander, alongside the Mara river, at the northern end of the Triangle. There are water plants, birds and animals, such as hippo and elephant, immediately nearby.

The tents look out over the wetland

Accommodation is in 17 large, permanent safari tents, all facing on to the wetland, each with its en-suite bathroom.

Food is served al-fresco when possible, but a large mess tent is also on standby for whenever it rains or the resident elephant, "Blossom" comes to visit. The food is international in style, and is usually served at the table.

The camp has a lovely, relaxed atmosphere, lit with traditional hurricane lamps every evening. There are birds and animals all around, so keep your camera ready.

Balloon safaris can be booked here and leave from behind the camp.

There are two airstrips: Kichwa 5-10 minutes drive, and Governors', across the river by ferry, 10 -16 minutes.

The interior of one of the traditional safari tents

Right: Time for a candlelit dinner

102

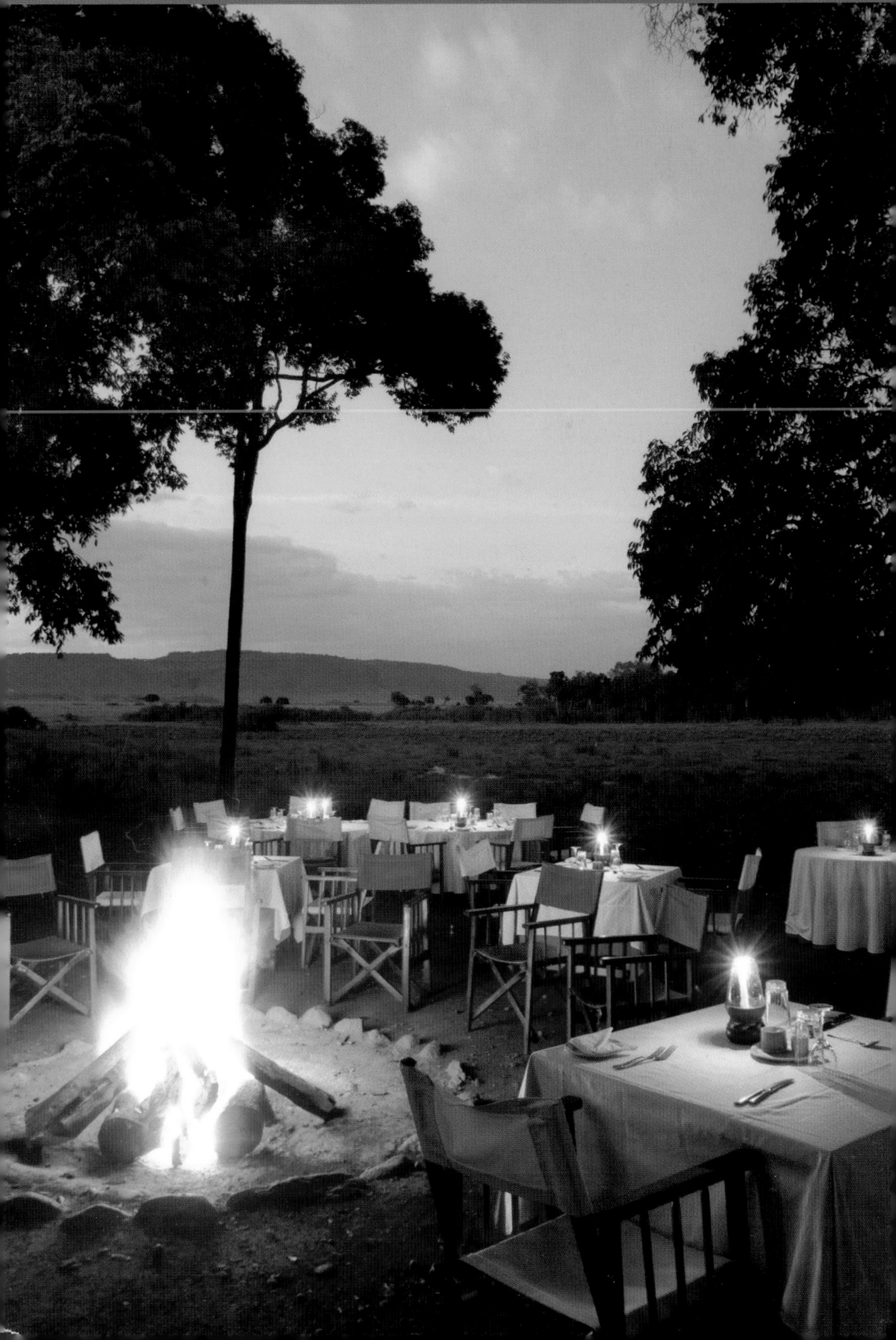

Camping in the Triangle

The Triangle has three public campsites and five private campsites. No booking is required for public sites, but bookings for private sites can be made using the Mara Triangle website. *www.maratriangle.org/visit/conservation-fees/camping*

Camp Security
For all camping, both public and private, all campers must hire two rangers for night-time security, as campsites are not fenced. The current fee for two rangers is KSh4000.

The emergency number for Mara Conservancy HQ
0729 120348, (8.00am -5.00pm) and 0722 740 338 (24 hours)

Iseiya public campsite

Public Campsites
There are three public campsites.
Oloololo Campsite, at the Oloololo Gate. Maximum 30 campers
Iseiya Campsite, near Mara Conservancy HQ. Maximum 10 campers
Eluai Campsite, north of Mara Serena Airstrip. Maximum 20 campers
Oloololo and Iseiya have "long-drop" toilets, and there are showers at Oloololo. Otherwise please bring your own water, and carry all rubbish away with you. Public campsites are available on a first-come-first-served basis.

Private Campsites
There are five private campsites in the Triangle, each of which can be booked exclusively for you to enjoy. For locations, refer to the maps on pages 4-7.
The camps are Dirisha, Maji ya Ndege, Ndovu, Olarro and Kiboko.
For booking, current fees and booking conditions, refer to the Mara Triangle website, above.

Accommodation outside the Triangle

Immediately north of the Mara Triangle are camps which use the Triangle as the principal area for their game drives. These include Kichwa Tembo and Bateleur, Mara West, Olonana, Mpata Club and Kilima.

Further afield, there are many options in the conservancies, which have their own game drives, but visit the Triangle to see the river crossings during the migrations. These include Mara North, Olare-Motorogi and Naboisho.

Colourful accommodation at Mara West Camp

Lounge area under canvas at Kichwa Tembo

Lodges, safari camps and the community

Conservation will only succeed when it also has a relevance to local communities. So most lodges and safari camps run community projects which clearly benefit local people in some way.

One of these is sponsored by Mara West Camp, located high above the Escarpment, over-looking the northern Triangle. The camp organises volunteers and has recently funded the building of a clinic and classrooms, as shown here at the village of Lolgorien.

High density primary school class

New classroom building by volunteers

Find out more

There are very many guides and books available, far too many to list. However, you will find it inspiring to refer to some of the literature before your visit, and also afterwards to check out those things which really inspired you. It is invaluable to have a good field-guide for birds, which are far too many to cover in this guide. Increasingly you will find the best place for up-to-date information is on the Internet and in social media.

Social Media

For the Mara Triangle
https://www,facebook.com/maratriangle

For Mara Elephant Project
https://www.facebook.com/ESCAPEfdn

For Masai Mara Hyena Project
www.msuhyenas.blogspot.com

For background reading:

Serengeti Shall Not Die: Bernard Grzimek. (the book which first inspired the author)
The Mara-Serengeti: A Photographer's Paradise: Jonathan Scott
The Great Migration: Jonathan Scott

For use in the field:

Atlas of the Greater Masai Mara: David Watson
Map of the Greater Maasai Mara: David Watson
Masai Mara Animal Checker: David Watson
Birds of Kenya and Northern Tanzania: Zimmerman, Turner and Pearson
Collins Illustrated Check List: Birds of East Africa
Signs of the Wild: Clive Walker
Friends of Conservation Masai Mara Ecosystem Bird Check list

Mara Triangle website

If you want to keep up to date with developments in the Triangle, log in to the monthly report.
www.maratriangle.org/connect/monthly-report- (month and year)

There are also other good websites. Best is *www.maasaimara.com*, run by Johan du Toit, who supplies a wide range of unbiased, up-to-date information on the Masai Mara.

Acknowledgements

Thanks go to the wide range of companies and individuals who, together, made this guidebook possible.

Our thanks to the lodges and camps which provided sponsored accommodation during the research for this guide. They include Mara Serena, Little Governor's, Kichwa Tembo, Mara West and Ashnil.
Thank you to Safarilink, who provided flights to and from Nairobi.

Thanks to the Senior Warden for Mara Triangle, Joseph Kimojino, who gave us a special insight into various aspects of the Reserve, especially on lions, and also provided valuable photography.

We owe a huge thank you to Sue Heath of Seiya Ltd, who not only maintained communications between the Mara Triangle and our UK office, but also organised the checking of files prior to publication.

Finally, thanks to Brian Heath, Director of Mara Conservancy, for his continued encouragement for our map-making and guides, ever since the inception of Mara Conservancy in 2001. He is forever positive and helpful.

Photography is generally by David and Rosemary Watson, except for the following.

Pages 14/15 ad 27	Dhruv Shah
Page 77	Daniel Beckwith
Pages 10, 16 and 103	Governor's Camp
Pages 29, 45, 52/53, 86/87 and 97	Joseph Kimojino
Page 82	Felix Borner
Page 46	Masai Mara Hyena Project
Pages 26, 104	Asuka Takita
Page 23	Michel et Christine Denis-Huot
Page 57 (grey-headed kingfisgher)	Sean Hartley

About the author

Follow your dream

Fifty years ago, at Easter 1964, David Watson read Bernard Gzrimek's book "Serengeti Shall not Die". As a direct result, the following September, he set sail for Mombasa aboard the liner SS Rhodesia Castle, to become a post-graduate student at Makerere University College in Kampala, where he met his wife Rosemary. During the first vacation, David hitch-hiked from Kampala, Uganda, to Nairobi, on to Arusha and then to Serengeti and Ngorongoro, where he camped on the floor of the crater.

Fifty years on he has written numerous books on East Africa, and together with his wife, has recently published the first, detailed maps of the Greater Masai Mara, the northern end of the Serengeti ecosystem.

Other publications by the author.

East African publications to date include the following:

Travellers Tanzania and Zanzibar
Hotspots Kenya: the Kenya Coast.
(Both published by Thomas Cook Publishing)

Masai Mara map-guide
Mara Triangle map
Ngorongoro map-guide
Amboseli map and guide
(Published by Jacana Media, South Africa)

Map of Lewa Wildlife Conservancy
(Published by Conservation Mapping)

Atlas of the Greater Masai Mara
Map of the Greater Maasai Mara
Published by Photoprint Scotland (Safari Maps Kenya)

YOUR NOTES

YOUR NOTES